HEARTREACH

HEARTREACH

The Ongoing
Project Dengke Story

Professor Mel Richardson MBE

Christian Publications International

*First published in Great Britain by
Christian Publications International, an imprint of Buy Research Ltd.
PO Box 212 SAFFRON WALDEN CB10 2UU*

Cover design by Justyn Hall at J8 Creative
Email: justyn@J8creative.co.uk

Online references cited in this book are correct at the time of publication.
Online material may be deleted or reassigned at the copyright holder's
discretion. Readers are reminded that such material may be transient in duration.

www.christian-publications-int.com

ISBN 978-1-78926-514-9

Printed in England by Imprint Digital, Exeter
and worldwide by Ingram Spark

Contents

It is my pleasure once again to commend to you this narrative of a wonderful ongoing story of adventure with a purpose. It is good to see teams of dedicated people using their skills, energies and talents to help others in need.

Sir Ranulph Fiennes Bt., OBE, DSc
Internationally Renowned Adventurer and Explorer

When many claim 'fake news', here is inspiring good news, from many for all!

Commodore Adrian Nance (RN rtd) OBE,
Formerly Commanding Officer Ark Royal Aircraft Carrier

After sharing the Word of God with the imprisoned Nelson Mandela when I was prison chaplain at the Robben Island Prison, he said to me "You give me hope". This same enduring message of a living hope in Jesus Christ resonates powerfully throughout this wonderful story of hope in this book.

Rev Colin Chambers Lt. Cdr. SAN, UED, Dip.Theol,
former Prison Chaplain, Robben Island
Maximum Security Prison, South Africa

Risk. Adventure. Into the unknown – sometimes into places and sometimes into strangers. Dr Mel found it in both, in an isolated village high up the mountains in China. He took life, health, reconciliation, friendship and Jesus. Read these living stories of how risk transforms.

Squadron Leader (rtd) Dick Bell MBE,
RAF Fighter Command Test Pilot,
Instructor and Aerobatics Champion

It is very encouraging to read of God's work being carried out in one of the most remote parts of the world. The fascinating accounts of people's reaction to the gospel shows how God's love can reach the hardiest of people. The project also shows how practical help can be an important part of Gospel witness. I hope the book inspires others to have a big vision for serving God.

Professor Stuart Burgess
B.Sc., Ph.D. (Brun.), C.Eng., F.I.Mech.E.,
Engineering Design Research Director Bristol University,
Former Asst Director of Research and Fellow of Selywn College Cambridge and European Space Agency

In all my years as a serving police officer, in every rank, I had surprises and nerve-racking experiences throughout. But on reading *Heartreach*, I have been deeply challenged and had cause to rejoice because every page has its surprises, its encouragements, its heart-throbbing moments and the thrills of serving God and seeing Him at work. Project Dengke – you may have to delve into atlases to discover that this is in China with Tibetan influence – with its ancient culture, its fear of Westerners, its primitive living – now wonderfully aware of the gospel and of the many who have now trusted the Lord Jesus – and the exhilaration of hovercraft transport on the River Yangtze. I found it very difficult to put down this brilliantly written account and you will, I am sure, feel the same. It is wholly inspirational and deeply challenging; it is momentous and victorious. As the writer and fellow travellers discovered, page after page is life-changing!

Robin Oake QPM former Chief Constable of the Isle of Man Constabulary and also Assistant Chief Constable in the Greater Manchester Police

Preface

Squadron Leader (rtd) Dick Bell MBE,
RAF Fighter Command Test Pilot,
Instructor and Aerobatics Champion

Devoid of all vegetation except tundra grass, the riverside vista of the top end of the river Yangtze Kiang in China/ Tibet is arid and brown. But it is stunningly beautiful. Everywhere that God has had his hand in constructing has a glory of its own, and the environs of that mighty river were no exception. Nothing seemed to live there. The grass was short and stubbly and seemed to be the only thing that yaks could eat. It also seemed to pass right through them because yak dung made an acceptable fuel for a night time fire. Dried, that is. The Tibetans stuck the wet stuff on the side of their huts to dry in the freezing sunshine.

There was no life. Oh, I forgot, we did see a group of wild horses one day. But we rarely even saw a yak. We knew they were there because one of our vets came in one day, bouncing up and down with enthusiasm – she had found a yak skull, complete with horns. We also knew that little brown eyes were peering at us from over the tops of the hills, wondering what on earth the noise was. No boats ever travelled that river – at least not up there. No sound of motors had ever tickled their ears. But when they saw a boat that floated above both the water and the land (a hovercraft), they must have wondered if aliens had landed. Not that they knew what an alien was.

The surrounding hills, at the time we flashed past, were pocketed with snow, some striped like a zebra. Of course, the tops of the Kola Shan mountain range were white, merging with the giant thunderstorms that chucked hail and snow wherever they pleased. That mighty river, tranquil and turbulent, tender and testing, snaked between the inundations to be the main road between isolated villages. But where we were, all civilisation had long disappeared. Only Tibetan tents and herds of yaks were seen, and those very seldom. Dengke was the last stronghold for people.

We set up our final HQ there, but away from the town and by the river. There was a haunting attraction to it. Altitude Tibetans have a culture that few know and few would understand. But humans, of all sizes and ages, know well the meaning of love. I call it "unconditional acceptance". At least, that is my definition of God's kind of love. It comes across in the eyes. And the smiles. And the warm offering of open hands. And, after only a short time, in a hug. And it works everywhere on earth. No matter that language is extra-territorial and unfamiliar, clothing is definitely odd and mannerisms inexplicable – love conquers all. That is what we had with the population of Dengke.

Some of us found the place and the people irresistible. Some came back. Again and again. One such was Dr Mel Richardson. There comes a time in one's life when we "gel". That is when we find ourselves in a place where our particular talents, longings and desires blend perfectly with a place, a people, a situation, a goal. We are a square peg in a square hole there. We belong. That is what Mel found in Dengke. He, above all the rest of us, "gelled" there. He went back.

He and his many teams set up medical centres, language centres, community centres and all sorts of other co-operations over the following years, bringing life, health and help to a forgotten and isolated people – but especially friendship.

And what else? They brought Jesus. Jesus was the

motivator of our journey in the first place. He engineered the permissions and the politics. He drove us ever onward and upward to achieve what we had come to do – to reach the source of the River Yangtze by hovercraft. He also stayed behind to open the eyes and hearts of a Tibetan community as to what a Great Big Wonderful God could do for them all. All the sons of Adam and the daughters of Eve are the same at heart: they all need loving and forgiving. That, at root, is what we all went to give, and what so many of them gladly received.

Introduction
Mel Richardson

Since my first Project Dengke book was published in 2002 much has happened including my first wife, Jackie, dying of a brain rumour. She left a letter to be given to me by Brian and Anne Williams in the event of her death. In essence, amongst moving and lovely words, it said "Keep going with Project Dengke heartreach and remarry as soon as possible – you need a wife!" The later thoughts were definitely not on my radar at that moment but God had other intentions. So it was, sometime later, another lovely precious lady called Ci Ci, now my wife, came into my life. Like Jackie she is clearly a gift from a loving God.

She spends hundreds of hours helping me, ringing up people, and making lots of practical arrangements such as booking hotels, hostels, vehicles and drivers, and generally encouraging me. My new young son, Kieran, plays his part too. Where would I be without them? You can read Ci Ci's story later.

Negotiations in China are often difficult, protracted and require not only someone who can speak Mandarin and understand the culture, but personal skills in dealing with very tough people. Ci Ci has all these qualities in abundance! She has been with me on at least 8 journeys into the mountains but in addition every year, every trip, she diligently helps behind the scenes. This is especially important when family commitments make it impossible for her to travel with the team itself.

This is my chance to say a huge "thank you" for always being by my side and supporting me through thick and thin.

The stories that follow would not have been possible without you.

Prologue
Mel Richardson

China and its state rules have changed radically in the last twenty years and we have changed too in order to respect and obey new laws. Currently, although we no longer run charity projects, we still enjoy visiting friends, family, and the gloriously beautiful tourist sites. Indeed, there is a big PRC government initiative to encourage tourism to these less well-known remote areas. Introducing our friends to the scenery, birds, flowers, wild animals and local culture is a great way we can help the local economy.

Many readers will be familiar with our first book "Nearest the Sun", published in 2002 as a testament to God's grace. In that book I wrote: "…watch this space…the story of Project Dengke is still unfolding. By the time you read these words the legal documents may have been completed and the next stage of fund raising and centre building may have begun. Maybe you will join us…maybe you will part of the story too…." It is no longer "maybe"! The Centre is built and a new generation of "tourist adventurers" have joined the team.

This new book continues to articulate ongoing "graceful" exploits with even more stories to bless and encourage you. We refer you back to the earlier book if you would like a "handle" on the full background.

Basically, hidden away on the Tibetan Plateau at a height of 3500 metres and 800 miles west of Chengdu lies the small town of Dengke. Situated in China's largest Province of Sichuan, and strongly influenced by Tibetan culture, the people are warm and friendly but often struggling with both a severe climate and medical deprivation. Happily, however, things have now got very significantly better as the years have gone by.

Following the British Hovercraft Expedition to China in 1990 and since 1992, I have led a regular series of adventurous teams to the area including one that unexpectedly got involved in a highly dangerous mountain rescue which was featured in the international publication "Readers Digest" and on the BBC TV series, "999".

By combining the scientific skills of Sichuan University (where I am a visiting Professor), my own Universities in Loughborough and Portsmouth, and companies across the globe, we have sought to share appropriate technology and expertise with the local people. Past collaborative projects have included: solar water purification, healthcare, eye and dental surgery, leprosy support and physiotherapy, eco-tourism, low cost satellite communications, bridge engineering using bio-composite materials, education and teaching, forestry, clean water supply, and many others. We set up a Friendship Centre in 2006 and the "heartreach" stories shared in this volume stem from this location where we now visit solely as tourist travellers and sightseers.

I suppose things originally "kicked off" for me in 1984. Following a talk on his latest expedition, Squadron Leader Mike Cole OBE wrote in my Visitors Book "Yangtze next stop – we need a plastics expert." Thus, began a series of adventures commencing with my appointment as Scientific Director and Deputy Leader of "The British Hovercraft Expedition to China 1990". This World Record breaking project opened my eyes to the potential of "Adventures with a Purpose" where Christians could build bridges for the gospel by using their God-given skills and influence to help those in need.

Dengke was the site of the first Hovercraft base by the side of the River Yangtze that we established en route to its Source. Prior to this in 1987, whilst on a planning "recce" in China, and poring over a German map, we decided to divide the first 1,000 miles of the river into equal stretches where fuel dumps could be laid down. Thus it just happened that the village of Dengke, later to become so close to my heart, lined up alongside the first of several equally spaced knots on a length of string conveniently laid out like a snake along the winding blue path of the river. Whilst camped just outside this same village in 1990, I was deeply moved when an old goatherd gave me one of his only possessions – a sling shot made of goat and yak hair. Likewise, a young urchin girl called Udren gave up her only toy, a beaten-up rubber ball, for Rob to give his daughter in UK. This extreme generosity prompted me to promise to the village that "one day I will return to help you." Thus, in setting up and leading/ planning many subsequent "Project Dengke" expeditions, I was keeping my promise!

Fulfilling this vow has brought great joy into my life and given me the pleasure of encouraging a whole new generation of dedicated young tourists from China, UK, and worldwide, to discover the beauty of creation and the joy of serving others in the name of Jesus.

SECTION ONE

PULLING NO PUNCHES

Chapter 1

CHAMPAGNE MOMENTS

In my previous book I wrote about "champagne moments" when things happen that are either exciting, extraordinary, or very joyful. Probably there cannot be any more joyful moment than when one of our interpreters comes to the Lord – maybe not immediately in the Centre, but sometimes a little bit later, and then they share their testimonies with us (see Section 2 "In their Own Words"). However, Dengke itself has been the location where the Lord has blessed numerous people.

Even going back to 1990, we had a member of the hovercraft team who was struggling to find out more about the Christian faith and whether he should commit. Clearly, the Holy Spirit was working in his heart and life. I distinctly remember one evening this particular guy came rushing in to see me, and his words were: "Mel, I have burned my boats!" I was not quite sure what he meant until he explained further: "I have let go and let God come into my life and I feel wonderful peace and joy in my heart already."

For many of us, that moment of surrender has particular significance and we remember it very well. In my case, I remember it was like the line of the hymn "My chains fell off, my heart was free". That moment of repentance and commitment and allowing the Lord to come in and take over is an indescribable reality. Given that this man had told me that he had burned his boats, I asked him to explain a bit more. The gist of what he said went like this: "You know that

I have been with you guys on the hovercraft team, I have seen you working together, I've seen that you are ordinary guys and that you don't always agree with each other. You're quite tough characters, quite adventurous, quite independent, but I have seen your Christian commitment and I have seen the way that you pray together and the crucial thing is I've seen how you disagree with each other." It was this phrase "I've seen how you disagree with each other" that was the key. It was not that we were always in harmony with everything but when we disagreed there was graciousness about how we described our disagreements to each other – and we tried to resolve them.

There is a verse in the Bible (John 13:35) which says "by this everyone will know that you are my disciples, if you love one another…." There is camaraderie, a kindness and an empathy that you can have for somebody even when they vehemently disagree with you.

Another example of a specific blessing that occurred in Dengke itself came some years later. I remember one chap whose name I won't mention since we will give his own testimony in due course, who had a problem back when he was around 12 or 13 years old when he had met a bunch of Christians. These Christians had told him that if he prayed a certain way he would be released from his diabetes. The problem was that they were mistaken. They had the best of intentions but the Lord does not always answer in the way that we think he should. The net result was that this particular young person gave up all his injections and drugs and very quickly became ill again. Now, unsurprisingly, he became disillusioned, and he carried this chip on his shoulder for a long time. By the time he came with us in the mountains I guess he was in his early twenties and he was clearly very challenged as he listened to various testimonies. During our devotional times, there were also several talks that interested him. I should mention that whenever we have devotions we do not pressurise people, they are purely optional. People do not have to come to any of our little Bible studies or prayer meetings. They are entirely at the discretion of team members. We have them every morning and sometimes in the evening as well. This particular man told me he was struggling. His typical comment was, "One day, I will become a Christian, but not now."

Imagine my surprise when he actually came to me and said he was ready to repent, believe, and commit his life and then trust in Jesus to go forward in the Christian life. I explained to him the basis of coming to know the Lord and I said to him: "I suggest you go and find somewhere privately to pray and respond to the fact that the Lord is already reaching out to you. He will meet you, and he will change your life." A little time later he came back to me and said: "Mel, I did all that you said and I don't feel anything inside. Basically, I don't feel that any change has taken place in my life." I explained to him that this is not about emotion. It is about accepting God's promises. But from my own experience and that of others, I know that even if there is no greater emotion there is very often a sense of peace that the Holy Spirit has come in. He said to me: "I don't feel any peace at all." This worried me. Back in my room, I prayed: "Lord, can you meet with him? What has gone wrong? I know that you bring peace and joy into life. What has happened here? I am sure he is genuine."

Then, in the middle of the night (it always seems to happen in the middle of the night), I got a spark of inspiration. Maybe it was aided by the peacefulness of the early morning, but I suddenly realised what the Lord wanted me to say to him. We had a private chat and I said: "Something seems to be on my mind. I need to ask you something. You told me that when you were young, you had this sort of false start with well-meaning Christians. They said you were going to be healed of your disabilities but it did not work out the way that you thought and hoped. Have you ever forgiven them for that? Have you ever recognised that they might have made a mistake? Have you ever felt that you can let go and let God deal with you and not harbour bad feelings for those well-meaning Christians that you met many years ago?"

He replied, "Actually, you have a point, I do feel a bit of a grudge. I still feel a bit upset."

I replied, "Can I ask you something? Can you go away peacefully and quietly and just ask the Lord to sort you out on this particular issue? Ask for forgiveness and realise that Christians make mistakes just like everyone else."

It was a day later I was sitting in the lounge of our Centre talking to an American (who, incidentally, was a former member of the US Navy SEALs, the elite, tough military group). He was a great chap with a great testimony. I was just fiddling with my guitar and talking to him, maybe he was singing something, but suddenly this other guy came in and said, "I have found it! I know it! I have a sense of peace in my heart. I feel like a new person. I believe the Lord has brought me into himself."

At this point, the ex-Navy SEAL said, "Well, man, give me five. Give me a high five, give me a low five!" I said the same. He did this and we were all very happy. Then he said to me, "When I go home and talk to my motorbike gang, the group I belong to, and tell them the first person that congratulated me on becoming a Christian was a Navy SEAL, they will all be amazed." Actually, this particular man was one of those folks who love to cover themselves in tattoos. It is not my cup of tea, I can tell you, and I am not overly keen on it but everyone has their own way of doing things, I suppose.

The next time I saw him, he extraordinarily had a tattoo

of Jesus on his chest, which I thought was quite amusing. I am sure that we are all aware that this is not a requirement of becoming a Christian. Of course, the real witness is a changed life, and for sure he now had a new life.

A Cry for Help

One of the great joys of being able to go back to Dengke from time to time, normally in the summer, is that I get more and more friendly with the local people, who recognise us and really could not be more warm towards us. Dengke itself is sort of split in half by the Yangtze River. We are on the Sichuan side of the river, and our visas enable us to go around there unimpeded. If we were to go across the river into the Tibetan Autonomous Region, strictly speaking we would need special permission. Through our friends in the police, or a local doctor friend, we can go and explore there for short periods if they come with us. From the mountain we can look back and take spectacular pictures.

A while back, we had two girls who came to see us in great distress and tears. They knew that in the past we had done a lot of humanitarian stuff for people in all sorts of ways. They were pretty desperate. They had come across the river and wanted to talk to us privately, which we allowed them to do. We found out that their brother was in desperate straits. He needed a kidney transplant and no one could help. We gathered that they had spent all their savings. They had even sold their most precious possessions and tents to raise funds for him to have medical tests and treatments.

It had come to the point where they said that the only thing that could help him was a kidney transplant. It was clearly a genuine cry for help, and to cut the long story short, we knew that this would cost a lot of money, even if they could find a suitable donor. We prayed about it, fully aware that it is not a good idea sometimes to give people cash.

Strictly speaking, we are not supposed to anyway, because the authorities are always worried that the money is going to be used for an uprising or for some other unlawful purposes or that the foreigners are going to be cheated.

In this case it was clearly an agonising cry from these two girls to their Christian friends who they knew were living across the river. Taking the story of the "Good Samaritan" Luke 10:29–37 to heart, we clubbed together and gave a few thousand pounds to help them to at least have the chance to take their brother to Lhasa to have suitable surgery.

On the way to the hospital he was so ill that they had to keep stopping their journey and, in the end, nobody could save him. It was right that we were able to do something to help, but knowing that they had sold all their possessions, we told them they could use the balance of the money to support their family and get their life back on track.

The Great Escape

In 2014, I was in the mountains in Kangding, and I was taken ill. My temperature went up to an extreme high of 41°C and all I remember was actually feeling extremely cold, but after that my memory is still a bit blurred. I was rushed back from Kangding to Chengdu and I told the team to carry on the project without me.

I was given lots of different tests and it turned out I had a serious gallbladder problem. I was taken to a VIP suite in a Chengdu hospital, which was both incredibly comfortable and expensive. Fortunately, I was already covered by my BUPA travel insurance. I was well looked after and the doctors were very good. I had tubes inserted in my arms and had various treatments, and slowly but surely was brought back to a normal temperature. Although the extreme pain had now subsided, I was advised to return to the UK to undergo an operation.

I get very bored lying around in bed as I am the kind of person who likes to be active all the time and rest is not something that comes naturally. My mobility was reduced, due to all the tubes, and I started saying to myself, "How can I get rid of this boredom? How can I have a bit of fun?"

My eyes wandered towards the window and, as I looked out, I could see a park where there was a pond with people milling around enjoying the sunshine. I thought to myself: "Wouldn't it be wonderful to get out of this place and take a walk in the park, even for a short while?"

So, a plan of escape started to form in my mind. Now, at certain times of the day I was left alone and there were no doctors around. Particularly in the morning, starting around 9 a.m. for a couple of hours, all was quiet. Doctors would do the rounds around 11 a.m. so I decided to devise a "recce". There were cameras dotted around and there was a regular schedule of comings and goings. I thought: "Knowing all this, how can I devise an escape plan?"

Remembering the epic war film *The Great Escape,* starring Steve McQueen, I mused to myself that if I were to get into that park unnoticed I would have to do a trial run. I requested a trolley from one of the nurses so I could connect my bags and tubes to it, allowing me to move around a little bit. I was given one, but they advised me that I should have someone with me at all times.

To be honest, by now I was feeling pretty well and I really did not need anyone else to help me. So, at an appropriate moment, I trotted off down the corridor, pushing my trolley in front of me. I looked around and I could see that nurses were asleep at their station. But as I went past one of them looked up, and was a bit startled when she saw me.

I politely said in my very best Chinese "Ni hao ma?" ("Hello – how are you?") and carried on pushing my trolley through the double doors ahead. I did not quite manage to pull that off as the nurses came charging down the corridor, shouting, "What are you doing? Where are you going, Professor? Let's get you back into the room!"

Back down the corridor we went. At the side of my bed was a bottle of sparkling water which looked a bit like a gin bottle. The nurses curiously started sniffing around it and possibly were beginning to wonder if I was under the influence.

By now, however, I had worked out when it would be possible to get out of this place and have a bit of fun. The following morning I went off, minus trolley and tubes this time, and sneaked down the corridor. I ducked down underneath the cameras and went past the nurse's station, then slowly down the stairs, knowing there was a security guard present at his desk. I am not sure whether he was asleep or absent but I managed to get out into the yard and walk across to the park. I was still attired in my stripy pyjamas. I guess I must have looked like an escaped convict or one of those prisoners in the Elvis film *Jailhouse Rock*.

I had a little walk around the park for half an hour, came back, and then let myself back into the hospital room. I was in bed just in time for the doctor's rounds. The doctor asked, "How are you feeling this morning, Professor?"

"I'm feeling a lot better actually. Thank you very much."

"Well, we still need to put some more drips on you."

"Okay, that's fine," I replied.

The doctor tubed me up. Then I thought to myself: I will have another go at escaping tomorrow.

The next day, having refined my escape plan technique, I crept out again. This time, I had an hour in the park. I went around by the pond and sat there looking at the flowers and taking in the "not-so incredibly fresh" air because it was in the middle of the polluted city of Chengdu. I sneaked back in and, sure enough, the doctors came around and said, "How are you feeling this morning, Professor?"

"Oh yes, I'm feeling fine again this morning."

"Oh good. Good."

Unbeknown to them, of course, I had been out and about without them "twigging". I repeated the adventure several more times in the park.

When it was time for me to leave for the UK, the hospital arranged for a BA flight to take me back, First Class, all courtesy of BUPA. The crazy thing was that a doctor from Singapore was flown in especially to be my escort even though he could not speak or read Chinese, which meant he had to get a translation of the medical report. We had doctors in my team who said they would fly back with me free of charge, but BUPA insisted on supplying and sending their medic. I did not complain because everyone had taken very good care of me thus far.

The doctor duly arrived, did all kinds of tests and commented: "They seem to have done a good job on you because you can walk around and you're obviously feeling a lot better. However, we need to get you back to England for that emergency operation as soon as possible because the gallbladder infection is going to return shortly if we don't do something quick."

On the day of departure, the doctor said that despite the fact that he knew I could walk, he had to put me in a wheelchair. I replied that was fine. He said, "When we push it up to the check-in desk, please look sad." These were his actual words. "Look sad, as they won't take it too kindly if you're going by first class and you look perfectly well." I was duly pushed in a wheelchair, even though I could walk. At the check-in I looked suitably sad. I was then escorted very slowly up the steps, by two nervous stewards who told me to "Walk slowly", and, "Be careful, Professor" and all that sort of stuff. I got seated in the plane and off we set.

The doctor was in the first-class module next to mine. He informed me he had to be with me at all times, even as far as the toilet door.

In the meantime, my family, including my little boy Kieran, were ushered to "cattle class" up at the back of the plane. I tried to "wangle" it so they could come in the first-class cabin as well, but the airline said they could not do that. Eventually, during the flight, Kieran decided he wanted to find his dad. He wandered up into the "posh" area, at which point he was shooed out by the duty steward. He said, "Is this little boy annoying you?"

"No", I replied, "he's my son. He has come to see how I'm doing."

Finally, after being looked after very well, I got off the plane and was taken home. The doctor did some more tests. It must have cost BUPA a fortune! Even the VIP hospital in Chengdu where I was staying had a suite of rooms and a TV in every one of them. Then there was the cost to fly me back and get me home – all very expensive.

On the original British Hovercraft Expedition to China that I was involved with in 1990, I had a colleague called Captain Gwyn Davis Schofield. He was a good friend and we did a lot of things together up in the mountains. He told me about his father who was part of the original Colditz Escape Committee as dramatised in the film *The Great Escape*, mentioned earlier. His father was the prisoner who escaped out of the German prison during WW2 hidden under straw in the back of a truck. If you remember the movie, the guard started sticking a pitchfork into the straw, trying to find any potential escapees. His father had managed to avoid the sharp prongs and escape. When I told Gwyn about my "escape story" he was very amused and told me that his father would have been suitably impressed.

Chapter 2

HE MUST BE JOKING

I was sitting in the Dengke Monastery (which many years ago used to be the King's Palace) with a couple of interpreters talking to the Rinpoche when he came out with an amazing statement: "I want my monks to become Christians." At this point I woke up, or at least started paying serious attention, and asked, "What did he say?" One of the interpreters repeated his words in translation and that he had said, "I want my monks to become Christians" and I thought to myself, "He cannot be serious, he must be joking." In any case, the conversation progressed, and after we finally came back down to our Centre, I started thinking: there is something not quite right here. This Rinpoche is a star celebrity speaker. He has got twenty thousand followers, has a big conference every year, is a well-respected Buddhist leader, calls himself "A Living Buddha" and he has just said to me that he wants his monks to become Christians.

Unbelieving, I then took another interpreter up to his monastery and asked the same question. I got the same answer: "I want my monks to become Christians." Still incredulous, I came back down to the Centre again and took yet another interpreter with me up the hill. The question was repeated and I got the same answer. Now there was no doubt in my mind. There was no mistranslation. He was serious. This was extraordinary.

It was not until many months later that I realised that on the very day that he had said this to me it was (and I didn't know it at the time) the World Day of Prayer for Tibet and the Buddhist world. Later still, after further months had passed, I had ongoing discussions which confirmed his sincerity. This was at a meeting with him in Chengdu when he pointed to his son and said: "I am particularly keen for my son to become a Christian." This was even more extraordinary. Then, over time, other statements came out from him, which can be verified by our interpreters, such as: "The best approach would be to share your Christian gospel with my young monks. They are more adaptable to new ideas."

Over the years, we have given him books to read about Buddhist monks being converted. Likewise, a dear brother called Frank Dunne always tried to keep in touch with him, an inspirational act which has proved to be crucially important in developing the relationship. Later, the Rinpoche made another comment along the following lines: "The first book you gave to me wasn't very impressive, but the last one really spoke to my heart." More conversations continued over a period of time and I made a promise to him that, if he really wanted, I could take his monks to Chengdu for lessons. We would call them "The Crimson Class" because of the colour of their robes. The idea was that we would teach them English and the Gospels using Bible stories, plus basic science and healthcare. I made this promise to him "in faith" that it would happen but I had no idea how it would work out. Certainly, at the time I did not know how we were going to do it in Chengdu or who we could team up with and the logistics seemed almost totally impossible. However, I just felt in my heart that I had to make him the promise – come what may! For what happened next I must pay tribute to others.

Later, I had more discussions with various great Christian people in Chengdu like Scott and a man called John G (not their real names) with whom I have now become very firm friends. We started to plan how we could get these monks into Chengdu for a week or two and we chose November as it seemed the perfect time. So it came about after a lot of planning and we actually got the Rinpoche and a whole load of these monks down from Dengke and into the Sichuan capital city.

Thus was started what I call a Good News English School (GNES) where a team of various local Chinese people and others from a number of church backgrounds teach English using Bible stories as their textbook. Some of my team were able to join in, including Carey (a Cambridge University physics graduate) who presented English and science lessons. Others taught songs and shared the gospel directly.

In that initial group that received the first lessons, one of the monks, I think his name was James, became a Christian and later left the monastery. Later still, he brought his brother to Chengdu to hear the gospel too, and as far as I know, he has come to know the Lord as well.

So this was a wonderful start to this particular style of ministry. However, things did not always go smoothly or totally to plan in the way that was first envisaged because I heard that the Rinpoche was a bit taken aback by how open and straightforward and honest the people were who were sharing the gospel. They did not hold anything back and I think he found it a bit hard to take. I do not think he was expecting these Christians to be so transparent and direct. Of course, we have to recognise that when the Holy Spirit stirs up the conscience and speaks to the heart then it can invoke a reaction of either surrender or of resistance. Truth can hurt.

Anyway, the group went back to Dengke and I was told that the Rinpoche had a bit of a hard time because the kids' parents really didn't like the fact that he allowed his monks to hear the Christian gospel. They felt they had seconded their children to his monastery to study Buddhism not anything else.

Later, he was visited by the police, or the authorities, and he had his passport taken away for a few weeks. Perhaps this was a bit of a warning that he was getting too close to foreigners. I often say to people that the Rinpoche is "treading on eggshells" so to speak, because of his desire to learn more about the gospel whilst at the same time getting a negative reaction from people around him, including fellow Buddhist leaders.

John G told me recently, very graciously, that he felt the whole movement to reach out to Tibetans that is going on in Chengdu at the moment all kicked off when the Dengke monks came down. Various groups of Christians from different church backgrounds in and around Chengdu were all wanting and waiting to share the good news in various ways. Suddenly, they all came together for a common cause and saw the huge potential. The wonderful thing is that, since that first class started, a whole string of other classes has continued so that now they have regular winter and summer camps and ongoing teaching and follow-up meetings. In one August there was a class of 30 folk learning the gospel through the teaching of English, and in the following January there was a class of about 70 students consisting of a mixture of both monks and ordinary Tibetans. The extraordinary thing is that all this is happening under the backdrop of increased persecution of Christians in China.

We know from first-hand reports and friends that many are being pressurised. For example, one of our young interpreters has been pulled in by the police two or three times to be interrogated, just because recently she became a Christian and wanted to attend a conference. Others are in the same situation of being watched, and we know that even law-abiding foreign Christians in China, including those in Chengdu and Kangding, are having their visas revoked or not renewed. There is an increased crackdown on worship anywhere other than in a three-self church set-up. We know that in recent years more than 30 Tibetans became Christians, which is a miracle because until now they have been considered to be one of the most unevangelised groups in the world.

All have taken baptismal classes and all have been secretly baptised, thereby witnessing to their friends. Seeing some of these baptisms take place has brought great personal joy to me. Recently, the very first Tibetan-speaking church was set up by local people in Chengdu. This is a very significant spiritual milestone. This little church is having a huge impact because the singing, the sharing, the preaching, and the testimonies are all in the local Khamba Tibetan language.

This helps to bridge the big cultural difference between Tibetans and Chinese. The Tibetans say that they are looked down upon by the Han Chinese and are treated more like savages from the mountains. Hearing something in their own dialect is incredibly important, and John G and his friends have got a music studio going and they are creating songs in this language. In China, there is the equivalent of "Spotify" (which we have in the West) where you can stream music with the full agreement of the local authorities. They are now streaming these freely available Tibetan gospel songs to communities across China. Effectively, they are downloading the "good news". They are getting up to 4,000 hits a day of people listening to songs and then responding and commenting. As you would expect, there is a wide spectrum of responses. Some people say, "This is a load of rubbish." Others ask, "What is this all about?" and other people say "This is wonderful! The songs match my own experience". So there is a vibrant evangelistic gospel conversation going on across perfectly legal multimedia platforms.

John G told me recently that they are working hard not

just on the main Khamba dialect but also subdialects. For example, there is a sub-group of about 5,000 Tibetans who have never had anything on multimedia before in their own language, never had songs, never had music or words, or audio files that they can listen to. John believes that the whole of that community will certainly be tuning in because it is unique to hear something in their own particular language. What a great ongoing opportunity this is – every single one of them potentially receiving the gospel message. As a past example, in the first year of operation digital analysis indicated that there were more than 500,000 overall downloads. In March 2019, there was a big "spike" and downloads rapidly increased. This seemed to coincide with one of the government's crackdowns on Christian groups. I am reminded of Psalm 2 and Proverbs 19 which say that God laughs at the plans of man and his ways always ultimately prevail.

Other extraordinary stories abound which serve to challenge and inspire we cosseted Western Christians who have things so easy. Friends of ours, Pastor D and his wife, were taking Sunday Service when there was a violent knock on the door and the police broke in and told them to disperse. He was preaching from Matthew 5: "Blessed are those who are persecuted for righteousness' sake, for theirs is the kingdom of heaven. Blessed are you when others revile you and persecute you and utter all kinds of evil against you falsely on my account. Rejoice and be glad, for your reward is great in heaven, for so they persecuted the prophets who were before you."

Pastor D said, "I respect your request but please respect me too and let me finish my sermon". Reluctantly they agreed. So, he sat them down in the front row and proceeded to share the gospel. As he came to the end the police jumped to their feet and said, "OK, that's it – move out," at which point he said, "Sorry, we haven't broken bread yet," and Pastor D proceeded with a final Communion Service. Undeterred, their church is currently continuing but it is split into 10 house groups each with less than 12 people all receiving the message and music by streamed video links which according to Chinese law is perfectly legal. In the weeks that followed the church continued to grow and they baptised 30 people in a secret river/lake location.

The Parable of the Dead Pig
On my team each year we have a wide variety of tourist and/or business people from all walks of life: doctors, nurses, unemployed, students, dentists, engineers, electricians, builders and professors. All sorts of folk and of all ages. I have calculated that something like 180 people have come with me from ten different countries over the years to join us as volunteers, all paying their own way and their own airfares and everything.

Amongst the people that have come we have had some real athletes, including a UK ironman contender. Likewise, we have had a retired member of the US Navy Seals (mentioned above). The strange thing is that sometimes the fittest people that we have with us have to lie down for a day or two once they arrive in Dengke. Maybe the bodies of highly tuned athletes need more time to adjust to the lower levels of oxygen than they have been used to at sea level.

To get to our destination, we have to go through mountain passes which are sometimes at an altitude that is close to 5,000 metres. Dengke itself is at an altitude of 3,500 metres, which is high enough for people to get altitude sickness. Happily, we have not had what I would call really serious trouble with that type of illness. One guy who came with us a year or two back was a world championship rower called Ben. He used to get me up at 6 a.m. to go out and do some training. I thought this was a great opportunity, away from my everyday life, to try to get some fitness back. Near the end of town there are 84 steps that lead right up to the school gates. Each morning we would go down there and start stepping 84 up and 84 down, up and down, up and down. In Ben's case, being an international athlete, he decided to run up and down but also run around the town then come back to join me as I completed a cycle – and to see how far I had got.

My early morning record stands at 3,360 steps. I would not say it was easy, but getting into the swing of it (or should I say the step of it) has certainly brought me benefits and I feel a lot fitter. Now Ben has instigated a new challenge. Following in the adventurous "footsteps" of Michael Zhang who some years ago cycled around the world in support of Project Dengke (see Appendix B), Ben and Lorro Reeves are planning to row across the Atlantic Ocean. I am so encouraged to have such audacious, fearless and brave people on our team. Brilliant!

Carey is the elder statesman on our team and he runs our early morning devotions and leads excellent Bible Studies. He told me on one occasion that every morning when I went out with Ben he held a meeting with the rest of the team (that is, when they eventually got up for breakfast) and prayed I would not get a heart attack! I am not sure whether he was joking. Once, going wearily up the steps, I was confronted by a sleeping pig that was lying across the stairs in front of me.

I felt this was a reminder not to be a lazy pig and I must keep going. Carey's interpretation of the incident, however, was that it was not a lazy pig but a dead pig reminding me not to overdo it and become a deceased leader! So, there you have it, one pig two different interpretations. The following year, Ben's brother Lorro came with me. He is also something of an athlete and kept the routine going.

Getting a Crowd

In our team, we have a wide array of talents. Most can gather a crowd around them. Typical of this ability are D and R. They are skateboarding experts and can do amazing tricks which to me look incredibly dangerous. They can flick boards, jump in the air, then land safely back on them. This is an incredible sight. They gather kids around, make friends and then share songs and stories. Their talent has enabled them to get some very interesting people skateboarding and we have pictures of a policemen, monks, and many others having a go. In some cases we have pictures of monks charging down a hill with their robes flying out behind them.

Others in the team draw bunches of kids around them by simply sitting down and playing a guitar. They love to sing and learn a bit of English at the same time. The older monks on the hill also like to play basketball. Whenever we are in Dengke we gather up some of these people, along with other kids, find a spot where there is a net, and then have a game. At the end of it, most people are exhausted, because remember we are up an altitude of 3,500 metres! Running around certainly takes it out of you.

For me personally, everybody knows I enjoy singing karaoke and playing my guitar – maybe not too well though, but I love doing it. I found this makes friends too, as it is almost like a universal language. One man who comes to see us whenever he can is a police sergeant. He also loves playing the guitar and after he or his officers have checked out our passports he starts playing along with us. Later in the evening he often returns, accompanied with his girlfriend and holding his own guitar, and we all have a sing-song. It is quite fun because he has got a peaked baseball cap which he wears as a policeman, and once he snaps on his guitar he turns his peak around and becomes a cool dude. Actually, this particular guy has written quite a few really nice songs about a former relationship with a girl that did not quite work out. Apparently, he did not keep any pictures but his memories are expressed in love songs.

On a number of occasions, we have had monks come down from the monastery to join us and have a sing-song. It gives us a chance to enjoy singing together but also to play and sing some gospel songs, which is our way of getting the message across. These monks have iPhones or the equivalent and can pull down karaoke songs for themselves. They seem to know all the latest hits, which I find amazing when you consider we are in a very remote part of the mountains. On one occasion when they were singing some Justin Timberlake and Justin Bieber hits I said to them, "Do you enjoy singing these songs in the monastery?"

They replied, "No, we're not allowed to do any singing like this so please keep this secret. Strictly forbidden!"

I then joked with them and said, "Your boss the Rinpoche is always trying to raise funds for his monastery and I think there is a way we could help him out."

"What's that?" they asked.

I replied, "I'll tell you what, why don't you record a version of a Justin Bieber song and I will ask Justin Bieber's agents to see if they are interested in doing a bit of promotion."

They said, "Hey, that's a good idea, we will put our Western clothes on and record something."

At this point, I said "Oh no, no, no, please do not do that because I want it to be more authentic with you wearing your robes."

This would be great fun if it went viral on the internet. The interesting thing is that we have heard – but we do not know whether it is true or not – that Justin Bieber has become a committed Christian and uses his concerts to share the gospel with people. If so, then that would be wonderful and will be an even more interesting link for these young folk.

Chapter 3

MEN IN THE SHED

It is an open secret that the one meeting in the week that I look forward to most is an early morning prayer meeting with a bunch of guys called "Men in the Shed" (MIS for short). We used to meet in a real shed and have bacon butties. That has long since gone because now we meet in the back room of Geoff Marshall's house or in my leaky motorhome. When the door is opened early on Monday morning I am usually met by a load of cats (very friendly, very nice) and one cat in particular. After a cup of hot coffee we get down to joking with each other and sharing some amusing moments. There is a real sense of camaraderie and fellowship. At the core of the group are Lionel, Geoff, Phil, Peter, Graham and myself. Several others come along from time to time. After a few minutes of banter it is usually Lionel who calls us to order and says: "Come on guys, what have we got to pray about?" Over the years, the amazing thing is that people across the world have got to know that we have this meeting, and they send us requests. Typically, I will say someone in Chengdu has requested we pray for something, and someone in the USA has asked that we pray about this, and so on. We feel a real sense of fellowship with Christians across the globe. Peter Cunningham, who recently but unexpectedly went to glory, often quoted Spurgeon: "Prayer is the slender nerve that moves the muscle of omnipotence." Likewise, he brought us quotes from C. S. Lewis. Perhaps, secretly knowing he was dying, he brought us an anonymous poem he thought we might like to share with friends that was entitled "Have You Thought About Your Soul?" Movingly, it reappeared at the end of the Order of Service for his funeral, which apparently he helped to put together. I have adapted it into a "12-Bar Blues" song in Appendix A. Like the "Men in the Shed", you cannot fail to be challenged by its message.

I always feel the presence of the Holy Spirit, even when coming to the meeting not knowing what we are going to pray about. Within a few minutes the Lord seems to press upon our hearts things which need to be lifted up immediately. Often, we find that the Lord has put upon our lips collectively the same situation or person to pray for. It is a joy to hear someone else praying the same prayer we were about to articulate.

We have had the privilege of being able to report back on so many direct answers to prayer. The Lord manifestly answers all prayers even if there are apparent delays, or if situations unfold more slowly than perhaps we would like.

I remember Geoff (now rejoicing in glory) praying fervently for myself and the team on Project Dengke and requesting along the lines of: "Dear Lord, please do something about the drunken mayor in Dengke who causes Mel so much trouble." This particular official had caused us so much heartache and trouble, year after year. Then, suddenly, he was removed in a way that was totally unexpected. Geoff's prayer very vividly came true. We heard that there had been a bit of an uprising in Dengke against some of the decisions the mayor had made. Although he was a Tibetan, he was very much working hand in glove with the worst elements of the Chinese local government officials (even though most are honest and honourable). The rumour is that he tried to stop a group of his fellow Tibetans from having a horse festival. I got the impression he was telling them that he would let it go ahead if he got some personal money out of it. Of course, I have no evidence. Anyway, the long and the short of it was that a big uprising occurred because there were half a dozen Tibetans arrested for protesting and there was a scuffle. The police and the army came in with guns and tried to sort it out as, by then, the whole of the village was demonstrating outside his office which, incidentally, is just about 50 metres across the road from our Centre. I heard that, as the fracas escalated, some people were actually shot and killed. Others were arrested unfairly, and for quite a while there was a lot of unrest. The net result was that the Chinese government, probably very wisely, decided to remove him from office. As my friend Glyn would ask rhetorically: is that a "coincidence" or a "God instance"? In my judgement, Geoff's prayer was directly answered and the mayor was kicked out. Now, a few years have passed and there is a new mayor, a new situation, and calmness in the town. Fortunately, most local government officers display integrity and veracity.

Going back a few years, when the old mayor was still in office, there was pressure on me to give up my officially documented rights to the Centre. Basically, only my name and Wujin's name are on the deeds (the reason for which I will explain later). The officials, including the mayor, were putting around a story that I had to surrender to Wujin all my official rights to the Centre or the government would take it over. This dubious deal suggested that if I did as they demanded then things could continue unofficially as normal but I would not have any official entitlements any more.

The pressures for this course of action were really strong, and for several years the arm twisting went on, but I resisted it. I just felt it was not the right thing to do. Some people even said to me: what a great opportunity – you could effectively demand money or compensation, and then put the cash into other Christian work or other projects. Deep in my heart I sensed the Holy Spirit's leading was to retain the Centre so that it could be used by local Christians as a "heartreach" base and also, I believe, one day as a Christian church.

Anyway, I dug my heels in and stuck to my guns, so to speak. The current situation is that we still have the Centre. The government is no longer demanding that we surrender it. It looks as though we are going to have the first ever Chinese Christian family group living there. This is yet another example of a wonderful answer to prayer, spun out of the "Men in the Shed". For many years we had been praying that this would happen, and in the Lord's time it has happened.

Chapter 4

LET ME GO AND BURY MY FATHER

In Luke 9:59-60, Jesus says to a man "Follow me" and the reply is: "First let me go and bury my father." That poignant excuse always comes to mind when I think about how the Centre, in its current form, was set up around 2006, as suggested or implied in my first book. It was finally built after many years of negotiating, putting pressure on officials and sheer persistence. How it ultimately came about is really quite a story.

It was not easy – in fact, it was very hard. It got to the point where eventually we got permission to build it, but only as a joint project. It had to be joint ownership between the UK side and the Chinese side because foreigners cannot build a Centre or a house in China on their own, and certainly not in this sensitive Tibetan Autonomous Prefecture. So, Wujin, the friendly doctor, donated the land to us and the idea was that we would then provide the money for the building itself, thus making it a joint project. But when the paperwork finally came through, and the red "chops" were put on the paper, I needed a team of people to sign with me to spread the risk. However, it was something of a heartache for me at the time that I could not get anyone to stand with me. I really felt so strongly that we should proceed, even though it meant perhaps putting our own houses at risk in England if something went wrong.

I asked if anyone would "do the honours" and put their name on the paperwork alongside mine and thereby "laying their heads on the chopping block", I suppose you could say. Sadly, at the time, everyone had wonderful excuses and genuine reasons why they could not do that. But – and it is a big "but" – what do you do if you feel strongly enough that something is the right thing to do? For me, it was a "no-brainer" – I was determined to go ahead.

I learned this from Squadron Leader Mike Cole when I was his deputy on the hovercraft expedition. I always remember him saying to me that sometimes we have to be brave and go it alone if circumstances demand it.

We always used to describe Mike as a guided missile – nothing would stop him once he was set on a course of action. We just had to make sure he was pointing in the right direction! Folks were saying to me I should not sign on my own. "Wait until you have got a good group of people who can stand with you to dissipate the risk," they said. I was unmoved. I was in no mood to back down, even though I was putting my own house, my reputation and everything else at risk. Maybe I would never be allowed back into China if something went wrong.

I remember the challenge that somebody once made to Mike Cole. He said, "Mike you are a great leader, and uncompromising about reaching set goals. But don't you think sometimes you are a bit arrogant? Have you ever taken advice from anyone?"

Mike, with a twinkle in his eye, paused, scratched his chin, and retorted: "Yeah, I did that once; it was a total disaster, I will never do that again!" Actually, I knew Mike well, and he did take advice, but sometimes as a leader you have to make unpopular decisions. I have learned that it is good to listen to all sorts and varieties of voices telling you to go this way or that, but sometimes you have to take the lonely path and do what you consider to be right, even in the face of great difficulty. So there it was. I signed. I decided to take the total risk for our side and that is what happened. Hence the reason why only my name appears on the paperwork. Now, as it turns out, in God's providence, that was exactly the right thing to do. In the current political circumstances most of the NGOs (which we are not) and groups of people that are working in China, particularly those involving foreign Christians, are being kicked out one by one or are not having their visas renewed. The fact that it is just my and Wujin's names (because we are not an NGO) on the paperwork stamped and signed by the government has proved to be an absolute "Godsend" in the true sense of the word. I can see now, looking back, that although I felt very disappointed at the time, the Lord had good reason for directing things the way He did. As we read in Romans 8:28, "And we know that in all things God works for the good of those who love him, who have been called according to his purpose."

Chapter 5

I AM COMING WITH YOU

In the course of leading Project Dengke I have had the
pleasure of meeting some extraordinary characters,
none more so than George Patterson. Some years ago,
international journalist Dan Wooding interviewed him
and was told how he left a small village in Scotland in the
1930s on a quest to find God. When George challenged
God to reveal himself, the answer was to to Tibet. From
that point he became embroiled in an adventure that was to
result in him not only finding God, but also in his helping
the Dalai Lama to escape to India. He was considered the
"Braveheart" of the Khamba Tibetan tribes. He learned
not only the Tibetan language but also how to ride, shoot
and hunt, Tibetan fashion. At the Columbus Screenplay
Discovery Awards, his book *Patterson of Tibet* took the top
prize. His film *Raid into Tibet* was awarded the Prix Italia in
1967. George met and married Dr Meg Patterson, a fellow
Scot, and the two of them went on to help rescue a number
of drug abusers, using their revolutionary detox treatment
called Neuro Electric Therapy (NET). As an aside, NET has
been revitalised, modified and updated by Dr Graham Giles
MBE, one of my early morning prayer buddies in the "Men
in the Shed" group. SPERA (Subtle Pulse Electro-biological
Recovery Apparatus), as it is now called, is currently getting
hundreds of drug addicts off heroin and other substances
– usually within a week, and without side effects. Totally

amazing! SPERA in Latin means hope – very appropriate!

Anyway, meeting George this charismatic 90+ year old one day in his Scottish care home, he told me: "Your book is by my bed, I pray for you every day, and I am getting fit to join you....." At this point he gestured towards a newly installed running machine in the corner! He explained that a lot of his previous adventures took place in the area where we go … so very appropriate. Returning to my church in Gosport, I decided to articulate to one of my elders, a GP, the dilemma that was welling up in my mind. I explained that to have this incredibly famous missionary on my team was a huge honour, but what if the Chinese authorities found out about his past escapades and they remembered they had put a price on his head? Even more to the point, what if he died on me!

The doctor asked, "Where do you think he would like to die?"

"In his beloved Tibetan Mountains."

"Exactly! Bury him by the side of the Yangtze."

In the end, before I had to make the final decision, George passed to glory. Notwithstanding this, it was a huge inspiration to me to have met such a wonderful, adventurous, faithful servant. We press on, effectively treading the same paths he once trod with such distinction.

Over 60 years ago, the Dalai Lama fled his homeland of Tibet on horseback because of Chinese persecution against Buddhists, and over thirty years ago he received the Nobel Peace Prize for being a messenger of non-violence.

Early one particular morning, as mentioned earlier, John G (with whom with others was initiated the Good News Bible School in Chengdu, teaching English using Bible stories), told me that something truly amazing had happened. The Lord was, and is, leading others independently in the same type of "heartreach" in other locations. Christians were doing what we had been doing in Chengdu and Dengke, now actually within the Dalai Lama's monastery in Dharamshala, India. Apparently, some people objected to this and informed the Dalai Lama, expecting the believers to be kicked out. On the contrary, however, he personally instructed his followers and the Indian authorities to "leave the Christians alone".

It is amazing how God works out his plans.

> I know that you can do all things;
> no purpose of yours can be thwarted.
> Job 42:2 (NIV).

The following chapters of testimonies will demonstrate this further. Read on!

SECTION TWO

IN THEIR OWN WORDS

Chapter 6

CAREY HARMER
CROCODILE CAREY

*People ask me why I call our much appreciated devotions
co-ordinator Carey Harmer "Crocodile Carey". Read on!
I always get him to pull out his matchbox of personally
extracted crocodile tooth trophies as a way of giving him
a great introduction. Here is his story complete with extra
fascinating insights from his wife Hilary.* — Mel

In my first job I saved up for a year at Bible college. I should
tell you that now I am an old fellow of 80. Unexpectedly,
the local authority gave me a grant so I had an additional
year as a freelance student. Arriving at the Alliance Club
in London, a Christian hostel for international students, the
manager suggested I should share with a Chinese student.
I had never met a Chinese person before, let alone shared a
room with one, but I said to myself: You go to missionary
prayer meetings – what are you worried about?

A Filipino pastor I was friendly with was staying in the
hostel. One day he said to me, "I hear the Chinese boys have
invited you to their party." I had accepted without much
thought. "You are the only white boy they have asked. It
seems God has given you a gift for getting on with Chinese
people." This was a word from God, encouraging my interest
in China.

At the beginning of my "free" year, I heard of a Chinese
course – highly unusual in those days – at Holborn Institute.
It was only three afternoons a week for a few months, but

they had a language laboratory – a new educational invention, with a microphone and headphones for each student, so the teacher could listen and correct each one individually. The Chinese lady teacher – she was a communist, and later tried to recruit me – taught me to speak with the tones of the Beijing dialect (the equivalent of "the Queen's English").

I thought of going to work in China, but this was in the days of the Cultural Revolution, and foreigners were not welcomed by Chairman Mao. So I got a job as a teacher in Sarawak, on the north-west side of Borneo, part of the newly independent state of Malaysia. English was then the national medium of education. I was appointed (at age 26!) Headmaster of a Junior Secondary School in the jungle, two days' journey up the enormous River Baram. Two years earlier, a military landing craft had off-loaded a JCB which drove up the bank and bulldozed a large clearing for the new school.

I had four teachers: an American Peace Corps volunteer, a British VSO youth, a Malay and a Chinese person, and 120 boys and girls, boarders, mostly from the local tribal longhouses, though some had travelled a hundred miles down-river from the mountains, and there were some Chinese pupils. As well as school matters like planning the timetable, I discovered I had to arrange for the purchase of food supplies, books and everything else. I knew nothing about anything, but God had provided a missionary family who lived in the village and spoke the tribal language. They told me to order rice and meat from the Chinese shops in the village, employ a couple of Chinese women as cooks, and announce that I would buy vegetables, which the locals would then bring in.

The local religion was 25 per cent evangelical Christian, and the rest Roman Catholic and animist. The missionaries told me that the Christian families were very pleased to have a Christian Headmaster. Soon after I arrived they asked me whether I would identify myself with the local Christians or the Europeans, many of whom were heavy drinkers. The point was that *arak* was the curse of the tribal people, and that when they became Christians they were set free and the longhouses were "dry". So I agreed to be teetotal, leading to occasional (but not much) embarrassment when I met other English and American expats.

I acquired a 42-foot long longboat made from a hollowed out tree trunk. With 33-HP outboard on the back, it was the fastest boat on the Baram. Going down the river for the post and supplies, such as a 44-gallon drum of petrol every three weeks, took three and a half hours, and back up the river four and a half hours. One time, I and the Malay man with me saw a dead crocodile half in and half out of the water, with three small ones feeding on it. As we neared the bank, the small crocs ran away and, parking the boat by the croc, I used a large screwdriver to hack out a couple of teeth. Fish snapped up the maggots that fell from the rotting flesh.

One day I was teaching when there was a heavy thump outside, and in a flash the classroom was empty – a durian had dropped from a nearby tree. Durian is a fruit the size of a football, much prized by the locals and some Europeans (including us) and strongly disliked by the others. The tree was so tall that the boys could not hit the lowest durian with stones, so they had planned to shin up the tree and attach a rope to a branch and pull it down.

They were quite surprised when I pointed out that if they did that there would be no durians from that branch next year or ever. They held the animist belief that nature is ruled by spirits, so there is no point in saving or working for the future because the spirits are malicious and unpredictable. The seasons are regular because God has made fixed laws for the natural world. That is taught in the Bible. It was one of the foundations of the scientific revolution.

I learnt about the harshness of life in a non-Christian society. It is difficult for us brought up in our (residually) Christian country to understand how life in a heathen community can be cruel, greedy and degraded beyond belief. Here is a mild, true example: for tapeworm (endemic in the jungle villages) tablets have to be taken for 14 days to kill every stage in the life cycle of the parasite in the human body. The shopkeeper, who is from a different ethnic group, knows that after 10 days the patient will be aware that the worms have been voided and will feel better, and he deliberately sells them in packets of 10 only. Animists do not believe in science, they just think the tablets have proved stronger than the spirits that caused the disease. A local Christian teacher explains it all to the children in a science lesson so they can tell their parents, and is beaten up by a thug hired by the shopkeeper.

At the end of a year, I was transferred to teach physics in a senior secondary school in Miri, a coastal town, for an uneventful two years. In a practical lesson, one pair of Chinese boys could not get their experiment to work. Wanting to make a joke and show off my knowledge of Chinese, I said, "The feng shui is no good just here." To my surprise the boys took it seriously and immediately began to dismantle the apparatus. This was another example of how superstition and folk religion are antagonistic to science, which is based on the Christian worldview.

At the end of two years, Hilary (who is English) flew in from India, where she had been working in a rural research establishment for the Leprosy Mission. "If you visit another house after dark, ask the watchman to light you, because of the snakes," she said. We were married in the Sidang Injil Borneo (the Gospel Church of Borneo). In those days, families could not afford to fly halfway round the world for a wedding, and I was the only person there that she knew. I had to make all the arrangements myself. Hilary's two years in India were her preparation for life in China.

We returned to England, set up home, and for 35 years lived a humdrum life, bringing up a family in a rural area where there were no Mandarin speakers. We could not afford foreign travel, and our children had little idea of our earlier adventurous lives. I continued my interest in China and had over fifty books about the country, and historical novels set there (strongly recommended for cultural background).

Age-related redundancy was in sight at 65. We had had financial difficulties in a recession, did not have enough money to buy a house, and our future was uncertain. We used to go into Cambridge sometimes to help with a class for Chinese students. One day, the Christian Chinese lady who ran the programme said to me, quite out of the blue, "Carey, I know you are interested in China. If you and Hilary would like to teach in a university, I can get you contracts immediately." Eight weeks later we landed in Chengdu. Our children, then grown up, were amazed by this sudden move.

We were met at the airport and taken to our accommodation, which was a long way from the university. The next day we were shown around the campus and taken back to our apartment. "Term starts in nine days' time. We will collect you. Goodbye." So there we were, entirely on our own, first time in China, with no idea where we were in a city the size of London. We did not belong to an organisation because you cannot join one in eight weeks, and we had no friends. But God was watching over us, and had been preparing us over the years.

We had the phone number of an Christian English woman who lived in China and was moving to Chengdu. We thought we would try her number. She turned out to be a fluent Chinese speaker, living only five minutes' walk from our apartment. At that time, foreigners' fellowship groups were private, but after a few weeks she recommended us and we were welcomed into her group of Christian workers for Sunday service and communal lunch. Here we also found help with learning our way around the city, the language and the culture.

Everyone discovers that in China if you say "Ni hao" they say, "Ni shuode hen hao", meaning: "You speak Chinese very well." But I noticed that sometimes I would get the reply, "Ni shuode hen qingqu." One day I asked my Chinese teacher what it meant. She said, "I will tell you the truth. Most of you foreigners who study Chinese, we can't make head or tail of what you are saying because your tones are no good. But in your case, although your grammar is poor and your vocabulary is limited, because your tones are good, we know what you are trying to say. That is what they mean." This was the result of my study thirty-eight years earlier.

All these were ways in which God had prepared us and arranged for on-the-spot help at the beginning of our time in China. Since we lived a long way from the university, we did not meet students out of class, but we met teachers on the school bus, and some of the older academics became our good friends. Some have come to the Lord. Even now, fifteen years after we landed in Chengdu, they give us a hearty welcome when we visit.

One day after lunch we made coffee and were sitting at our desks, which were next to each other. Suddenly my coffee spilt. I thought Hilary had accidentally knocked the desk at first but it soon became apparent that it was an earthquake! We went into the lounge and sat down on the sofa together. The building shook for two whole minutes, and a flowerpot fell off the tall aircon unit.

When it stopped I looked around. There were no cracks in the walls, and the buildings across the street appeared to be undamaged, so we decided to stay quiet and pray together, and not rush out into the street. After an hour or so, an English friend of ours in his fifties came round on his bike, through the panicky streets, to see if we were okay, and then went on to check on other friends. Meanwhile, we later heard, the younger Christian workers were huddled together "sharing their feelings". Can you spot the real missionary spirit?

Large numbers of Chinese Christians and quite a few expats flocked from all over China to the disaster area to help. I taught in a Christian tent school on a huge temporary campsite for three weeks. The government was taken by surprise by the huge number of volunteers, the majority apparently unorganised Christians, who turned up to help after the Sichuan earthquake. Now, when an earthquake occurs, a military cordon is put around the area, so that will not happen again – an insight into Chinese government thinking.

Teachers are greatly respected in China. One day we got a message that the local military base invited us to make use of their shower facilities – the male teachers one day and the female teachers the next. An army bus took us to the base. Just outside was a purpose-built shower truck, parked by a stream. In the truck a heater heated the water to just the right temperature. There was a dressing room, and a shower room with half a dozen nozzles. The soldiers were amazed to be chatting with a foreigner in the shower. This was my weirdest experience in China.

One summer we went on a Chinese Christian "camp" for secondary school students, held in a school. One afternoon we took the teenage boys and girls for a walk up the local mountain. Stopping for a breather by an old temple (fortune-tellers often hang around them) I asked one of the girls if she would like me to tell her fortune. She eagerly held out her hand. "Oh, you are lucky, you will marry a rich, good-looking man and have two baby boys!" She beamed. Her friend came by, and hearing that the teacher could tell fortunes, offered her hand. I gave her an identical fortune. The first girl was very surprised. I told her I was just joking with them – they were easy to deceive, and that God determines the future and fortune-tellers are cheats. An acted story with a little bit of Christian truth.

Each year our university renewed our one-year contract, but the last half of our third year was cancelled by the government without any reason being given. So I became a full-time Mandarin student at a university in Chengdu, and Hilary worked for a Christian organisation. I was very pleased as I had always wanted to be a language student and study more Chinese.

In God's providence, these two years' Chinese study (you need four to become fluent), plus the knowledge of the city, and Chinese ways that we had acquired, came in very useful when our five years in Chengdu came to an end. At a conference in England we met Mel and Glyn, and I was able to join the Dengke Project (DP).

The DP uses Chinese translators with good English, so was my limited Chinese of any use? Well, here are a couple of stories. Chinese people are not into DIY, and on one trip I used to buy the building materials for each day's work from a cramped little hardware shop, nothing like B&Q. One day, two of the team with a translator went instead. The shopkeeper's wife said to the girl: "Where's that old man today? He doesn't wave his arms about and we always know what he wants." A language student gets a big boost from a remark like that.

I really admire the young women who volunteer as translators. They are usually city girls, and to them mountains are places of danger, not adventure – although Happy sent me a postcard from the base camp of Mount Everest, she was an exception.

Tibetan men carry knives, and are bigger than Chinese, who they think of as enemies (with some justification); scary for a Chinese girl. She might be unused to being with several Englishmen at close quarters, and embarrassed if she doesn't know a polite way to get this huge fellow (he is much older than her, and you should not boss older people about) to do what she wants, or discourage him from acting in an uncultured way.

In Dengke, going out of the Centre early one morning, I met a teammate and a translator coming in, having failed to buy breakfast for the group. The small eatery was crammed with villanous-looking Tibetan men – no wonder she had not liked to go in. I knew that as a Westerner I was quite safe. I went into the room and saw that the ten or so tables were all full. I nodded to the men and walked casually through to the kitchen at the back where, as I expected, there was a middle-aged Chinese woman and a girl hard at work. I said I wanted 20 hard-boiled eggs and 20 steamed rolls. She told me to wait a bit. I went back into the room and indicated I wanted to sit down, so the men shuffled along to make room. I said, "Tashi deleh" ("Hello" in Tibetan) and got some friendly smiles.

Five minutes later, the woman beckoned me into the kitchen, and counted the items into bags. I demanded pao cai (pickled turnip) which should have been included free; she looked surprised and put some in. I paid and went back to the Chinese part of the team breakfast. (There are now modern shops and cafes with Wi-Fi in Dengke as well as the old-style ones.)

Tibetan monks greatly fear the spirits of the mountains. They are always giving "blessings" for which they expect an offering in cash or kind in return. My response is a bit different. I take his hand, smile and give him this Christian blessing (in Chinese): "May the God who created the big mountains bless you." Yes, with God's help I did do a few useful things on the DP. You can see how I can say in the words of Jacob at the end of his life, "God has been my Shepherd all my life long."

Hilary writes
I was not able to travel to the mountains, for health reasons, but in December 2016 was able to welcome the party from Dengke to the start of the Camp in Chengdu. Here is how it came about.

Carey and I went to Chengdu in August 2004 to teach English at a university, for students who had not managed to get into a first-rate university, and were paying to be there. At the age of 65 I had never taught before, but soon got the hang of it, with Carey producing the lesson outlines. In the second year, one of my students from year 1 came and listened at the back one day. Then he told me I was much better than I had been the previous year!

Both of us had lived in Asia before and neither of us experienced culture shock in China. Being white-haired we were respected and looked after, and nearly always given a seat on the bus. In the first year, on Sundays we met with an expat group which we later joined. All of us had prayer partners, and mine was a young woman who spoke Mandarin and was learning Tibetan. I met a number of her friends in the city doing the same, and became interested in Tibetans and the way Christians befriended them.

In subsequent years we attended an International Fellowship in a large hotel room. Every week, visitors and newcomers were welcomed. One week, a group of wacky Brits who were just passing through were introduced to us. A year or two later, back in England, we were sitting around at a conference at Swanwick when one of these wacky Brits walked past! It was Glyn. He and Mel were setting up a stall to publicise the Dengke Project. Next to them, Doctor Ray was advertising her Blue Sheep shop in Chengdu. She was one of the members of the Yangtze Hovercraft Expedition who went to the source of the river in 1989. Carey had not been able to go on that expedition. Now Mel assured him that he was not too old at 72 to join the Dengke Project, and signed him up for that year. He has since been six times.

My role during those times was to keep in touch and encourage him, and to send on his letters to a group of friends. In 2015, I went out to Chengdu at the end of the project, and joined the team activities, including two meals hosted by the Rimproche, wearing a Western suit. He sang us a Tibetan welcome song.

The next summer, things started to move in Dengke. The Rimproche, who twenty years earlier had not wanted any contact with foreigners, asked Mel to arrange for some of the boy monks to have teaching in English, Mandarin, Healthcare and Christianity. Some expats in Chengdu agreed to make suitable arrangements. The result was that a four-week course was arranged for the monks from Dengke, with practical help from two house churches, and teaching by Tibetan-speaking expats. Mel asked Carey and myself to accompany him to Chengdu for the start of the course.

We arrived a week before the monks were due, and the first evening went along to the apartment used for meetings by one of the house churches, where the classes would be held. We met some of those who would be running the course, a number of the expats we knew and a young local couple who were our good friends. That was very encouraging.

The coordinator for the Crimson Classes, as the course was called, was a young American. A Korean pastor's wife and a Chinese woman, two very dynamic ladies, were in charge of the practical arrangements. We went with them to inspect a nearby apartment, which they agreed to rent. The contract would be signed the next day, when the monks were due to arrive. As the place would need cleaning and preparing, the monks would be accommodated in a hostel for two nights. They also hired a cook to prepare their meals.

On the Friday evening some of us met together for a meal with some of the Dengke interpreters who had come in specially to help. On Saturday morning we were all ready for the arrival. The Rimproche and thirteen young monks arrived safely and we all went to a hotpot restaurant near where the classes would be held. They all had very short hair and wore long dark red robes. It turned out that four of the monks were girls. We had a meal together and I was interested to see how seamlessly the interpreters worked to enable Mel and the Rimproche to converse with each other. The monks were taken to the hostel nearby.

Between the house church members and the expats, these young people would be looked after twenty-four hours a day. The coordinator himself slept in the apartment with the boys, and the four girls who came were welcomed into the home of an American family. Each day they spent from 9 a.m. to early evening in the classroom, and meals were brought up. In the evenings there were things like guitar classes and games provided. At weekends there were no classes, and they were taken out by various expats.

The local church people took us all to a restaurant for a meal. Although the area of the city they were in has lots of Tibetans and plenty of monks in the streets, a group of teenagers in robes would be very conspicuous. By Sunday lunchtime, when we all ate together, the Chinese Christians had provided them all with normal clothes. Later that day, Mel had to leave Chengdu, but Carey and I stayed on to see the classes get under way.

There was a storytelling in progress when we arrived on the Monday morning. Each word was said in Tibetan, Chinese and English, and repeated by the class. In this way they gradually learnt the story by heart. It was slow and patient work. We were looking at the teachers over the backs of the monks. It did my heart good to see a man whom I knew, who had been learning Tibetan for many years, now able to tell Bible stories to a group of young Tibetans. This class went on for most of the morning each day. The first week's lessons were from Genesis, covering Creation and the Fall. The next two weeks were about aspects of Jesus' earthly ministry, and the fourth week his death and Resurrection.

The cook arrived and brought a trolley up in the lift. There were large containers of rice and another dish, which were served out to everyone. During the break for lunch it was good to see these young people just being teenagers together, and enjoying the chance to learn new things. The majority of them would not have been in a city before, would not have been treated kindly by Chinese people, and would not have been at close quarters with white foreigners. The experience of being with Christians all the time for four weeks must have been amazing for them.

One lunchtime, Carey and I took two girls and two boys for a ride on the Metro. Construction of the system began in 2010 and has been expanding ever since. We rode to the large square in the city centre, had a brief look round and went back. They all seemed to have enjoyed the outing, and wrote their names for Carey in Tibetan and Chinese script. They all had an English name too.

The afternoon classes were in English: basic health and hygiene, and Chinese. Doctor Ray did the health ones, and as she spoke through an interpreter, we heard what she said. It was very illuminating. On two afternoons, Carey gave a science talk instead. On the second occasion I was sitting at the back of the room, and the Rimproche was on the other side, talking with a Christian Chinese woman. He speaks Chinese but no English. She came over to me and said that he would like to be prayed for, and would I come. He was sitting on a chair. We both put our hands on his shoulder and prayed, she in Mandarin and I in English. What a privilege!

At the end of the first week, Carey and I said goodbye to them all and returned to the UK. We heard later that at the end of the four weeks the leaders felt that one boy was very close to believing in Jesus. He subsequently left the monastery but we have not been able to contact him. Some of the others were also very interested.

These are the encouragements that I received from being there. Some of our long-standing Chinese friends were involved. Chinese Christians were beginning to engage in cross-cultural outreach to a minority group in conjunction with expats from various countries. Men who had spent years learning the language had a willing audience of Tibetan people to tell the Bible stories to. They all gave selflessly for four weeks to care for a group that they did not know, at Mel's request. We felt privileged to have seen a little of what was happening.

Subsequently, the apartment they rented was used for further "camps" as part of their ongoing efforts to reach out to other groups they have contacted. There is also a training course for local believers to learn cross-cultural evangelism.

Chapter 7

PACIFIC
BLESSED ARE THOSE WHO ARE PERSECUTED

Names here have been changed for their protection. This dear young "sister" has been called in and hounded by the police several times because of her faith. She loves her country and her leaders and it is manifestly unfair how she has been treated. In one interview she was told her mother was ill in hospital through worrying about her. On rushing back to find her it was revealed to be a cruel lie. Mum and Dad begged her to give up her Christian faith, find a lucrative job and marry as soon as possible. As a very attractive girl she has many admirers – just having a boyfriend or partner would be easy for her. Notwithstanding this she told them "marriages are made in heaven – I only want a Christian guy...." – Mel

Hello everyone, I am Pacific, but this is not my real name. I am really happy to share with you my stories associated with the Dengke team. In the summer of 2016, I was invited by a friend to join a team to go on a trip with some English-speaking people who were going to the mountains. They were clearly tourists who travel and help local people. Little did I know however this was a very special invitation and would make my life different.

First Meeting
In late July, the team gathered for the first time in a hotel room. I was late so there were already people when I arrived.

Team Leader Mel (I jokingly call him "Captain") said a phrase in Pinyin to introduce himself, which I struggled to understand until he said it in English: "crazy professor". Then everyone made a self-introduction. I could not remember much about each person's profile, because I was a little bit overwhelmed by all the strangers who all came to be unique and dear friends to me after the trip. I appreciated everyone being so friendly, smiling and greeting me naturally.

Daily Devotions

Every morning, the team gathered for a brief session during which we listened to some Bible teaching. I liked Carey's stories, which were used to lead into, or to illustrate, a piece of teaching, which made the information easier to understand. Although I don't now remember any of the stories in particular, I do remember I loved them.

After the Bible teaching, the team discussed things to be aware of, exciting news to share, and prayers to do together. I was not a believer and Mel told me I did not have to participate at the meetings if I would rather not do so. I appreciated it because I felt respected, and I chose to be at the meetings. I was amazed by the team's calmness when they were confronted with troubles. They were not worried but just shared and prayed together. Also, sometimes scriptures were shared in the team even on the vehicle when we were travelling on the roads (and often with bad road conditions). I liked the unity of the team, bound by their faith in the same Lord. That unity was built on hope and love. I sensed the beauty of their faith, even though I did not understand it back then.

Sharing Daily Chores

After we arrived in Dengke town, we lived in the Friendship Centre. The team was divided into pairs to share daily chores in turn. That was great fun. Different people cook in different styles, and we could have diverse meals from different food cultural backgrounds. Buying ingredients to cook meals, or booking tables in the restaurants for the whole team, required well thought-out planning and patience. Sharing tasks with partners also required mutual cooperation and tolerance. Meal time was a good opportunity for us to share news and invite local friends to join us. All this teamwork, with each member's devotion and love for the big family, really impressed me.

Prayers – Zhuoma and her Family
Every morning during daily devotions, there were prayers. I did not pray but I listened, though I did not quite understand, most of the time. In those days, we also met some local friends, and there was one occasion I remember particularly clearly when my friends prayed for a little girl and her grandma. We were hiking and heading back to the Centre when we met this little girl Zhuoma and her younger sister. They were picking wild berries. It was during early afternoon when the sun was shining brightly and the girls had been picking for some time. We could see they were soaked from the heat. I wanted to buy her berries and she invited us to her little wooden house. On the ground floor were a few cows and horses. We climbed up a wooden ladder to the upper floor where we were hosted and given hot water and steamed buns. Then we met her grandma. She had been sick and was thus confined to her chair. Brother John and Brother Chris asked her if they could pray for her. She said yes and they held her hands and prayed for her. That was the first time I have ever seen people pray for a sick person who was a total stranger. I did not catch what they said, but I was really moved. Two years later, I had already become a believer and there was one time when I prayed for an old

grandma begging at the street side. By then I did understand the two brothers' hearts when they prayed for Zhuoma's grandma. Actually, one of my students who saw me pray for the grandma said he was amazed that we (Christian people) did not choose to give her money, but to sit next to her, hold her hands and pray for her. I thank Father for his love which motivates us to love people, not in the way this world expects, but in his way, with the love He gives us.

In the summer of 2017, when we returned to Zhuoma's house, we prayed for her grandma again. She still remembered us from the previous visit and enquired after our friend who was not there. I know she may not have understood what we said, but she knew we loved her and was happy to see us. Zhuoma is now in university and has become a dear sister to me. Her grandma has often been ill. I hope to see them again soon.

The Young Monk on the Street

One day when we were buying things in the street, we came across a young monk. He was really hospitable. He said he would run back home to fetch something and made sure we waited for him. He returned with a kettle of butter tea. He offered us the tea and we sat together and talked. He said that Brother Chris looked like his elder brother who was killed in an accident years earlier. Poor boy. He really liked Chris.

Then, one evening, this boy came to our Centre. We invited him onto the roof, talked and watched the mountains in the distance, and the sunset. I was not patient, because I thought the conversation wasn't particularly interesting. But now when I think of it, it must have meant a lot to him, for that might have been one of his few chances to hear and to be heard. The next year, I went to the boy's monastery to visit him, but unfortunately I had just missed him. He had left the day before my visit. Brother Chris had given him an

English name, Paul. I wish to see him again and witness his transformation in the future. Now we look up to God's glory.

Young Monks at the Monastery
There was a monastery in Dengke town. After decades of praying and waiting, the Rinpoche agreed to open it to us. We could teach lessons to the monks. There were about seven teenage monks and several nuns, in addition to about twenty children. Normally, kids were sent to monasteries at a very young age to live and become disciples of the Rinpoche. Their families often think it an honour to send them to the monastery, considering that if they become learned monks in the future they will receive proper respect and often economic security in society.

However, the monastery was more a "woundland" than a wonderland for the kids. They were fed and put to bed, but they were not tenderly cared for. Many of them needed something as simple as a hug. We were so blessed to spend some time with them. We played games with them and taught them languages. Each one of them was unique. One teenage monk called Baima was very smart and honest. He joined us one night for karaoke and turned out to be a great singer. We all liked him. As for the younger kids, some of them were quieter and others naughtier, all with different personalities, but they all loved attention and company. We gave them football lessons, and they were running and yelling, full of energy and life. I remember there was one time when we were teaching them to draw. One child was copying from the board but was struggling. Then he decided he could not do it well and turned to me for help. I am by no means an art person, but I couldn't refuse a child. So I held his hand and drew together with him. My drawing was actually more terrible than his! But he did not complain and reject my help. I think he liked the attention and even just being held close.

In the last class we helped the kids cut their nails, brush their teeth and wash their faces. They were so obedient, doing everything joyfully as told. When I was cutting one child's nail, I accidentally cut his finger tip. I immediately took care of the small cut. Still, I felt sorry for him and thought he would not let me do the rest of his nails. But he did. And he did not complain at all. I was so glad that he chose to depend on me even though I was clumsy. I thank Father for those precious little ones.

This year, the local government took the children out of the monastery, and hopefully has put them into local schools. That is great news for them. God bless the kids.

My Transformation

In 2016, I joined the Dengke team and travelled to the mountains. I did not know then that the team, the things that would happen on the trip, and the people we were going to meet in the village, were going to change me, or that the invitation to join the team was a special invitation from God for me to get to know him. I thank God that his mercy led me to the team and to witness faith, love and kindness in his people, towards the least, poorest and most forgotten. In 2017, when I was baptised, I did not know how to live out God's love, but Father gave me opportunities to learn from brothers and sisters – to work with them as a team and family. Also, compared with what little I have done for the people, they have done so much more for me. They let me see God's awesome creation and his endless mercy on his children. I also want to thank my brothers and sisters in the Project Dengke team. Every one of you lives out God's love, tenderness, humility and generosity. In particular, your love and encouragement to me when I was setting off on this path of faith has meant a lot to me. I want to share a scripture:

"Dear friends, let us love one another, for love comes

from God. Everyone who loves has been born of God and knows God" (1 John 4:7).

I want Project Dengke to continue to be a blessing and witness of our heavenly Father's love over all nations and all people. May his kingdom come and his glory fill every place.

Chapter 8

JOHN GLASBY
A BUILDER'S TALE

John is one of those cheerful, friendly people with a heart of gold. Great skill, great commitment, always ready to share his faith. It seems he can "fix" anything. Several people in our current team can testify to being blessed hearing his testimony. – Mel

After participating in a three-week trip to south-east India with our church in February 2002, doing teaching and preaching in the Bible school and in the villages, God gave me a heart and desire for short term-mission and a passion to return to India even though preaching is not one of my greatest gifts.

Then, in September, Janet and I attended a mission conference in Swanage led by Frank Paine who was hoping to get volunteers to go out to Kazakhstan (which I got involved with a few years later). At the start of the first meeting we were asked to say who we were and what organisation or country we were involved with. As we went round the room, a lady (Sue Wernham) stood up and said, "I'm here on behalf of the Jin Hua Foundation in China." At that moment I was prompted to go and introduce myself to her. But, being who I am, I wrestled with that all weekend, thinking: is it from God or is it just me? Then, after the last meeting, when everyone was packing up their things and going for lunch, after plucking up the courage, I finally went up to Sue and said, "Hi, my name is John Glasby and I'm a builder."

Her response was: "We need teachers, not builders!"

"Well, maybe it's my wife that needs to talk with you, as she is a teacher."

So we had lunch and then went our separate ways, and I was thinking: "What was all that about?" We did not think about it again until I received a letter from Sue a few months later, saying: "I have a friend (Mel Richardson) and he has been involved in a project in China and is looking for a builder to help, and you came to mind, so here are his contact details. Maybe have a chat with him." Hmmm, maybe it was God after all. At this time I was thinking: my heart is for India, I have no desire to go to China. But God had other plans for me.

I called Mel after a week or two to introduce myself and he sent me a copy of the book *Nearest the Sun* and invited me to come down to Portsmouth to a China day at his church. So a few weeks later I went down to find out about the project and learnt that he had been given an old cinema to convert into accommodation for teams who go out.

I can remember driving home and thinking: OK, God, if you want me to help, what do you want me to do? I know: raise some money. So the following week I announced at church that I was going to do a sponsored diet and lose a stone in four weeks and people could sponsor me. I raised £230 for the project.

A few weeks later, Mel called me and asked if I would like to come on a recce to Dengke to have a look at this old cinema. This was March 2003, when God really put China on my heart. I saw the medical and spiritual needs of some of the poorest people in this remote part of China, as well as having the adventure of travelling three or four long, bumpy days along some of the world's worst roads to get there.

2003

With Glyn and Mel, I travelled in a 4x4, and on the road between Sirque and Dengke our Jeep ended up on its side after falling through ice into the edge of a frozen river. Despite this setback, we eventually got pulled out and arrived in Dengke which looked like a town in the Wild West, with Tibetans on horseback and gathering around small shuttered openings that were the local shops. I remember Mel asking me on our return journey what I felt about the project, and my saying "I don't think I'm qualified for this."

Mel replied: "That's great, neither are we!"

This was during the SARS scare and one time we were stopped at one of the many checkpoints, and a man with a spray can asked us to step out of the Jeep and then proceeded to spray the whole Jeep inside and out with what smelt like bleach, while our temperatures were taken.

2004

This was probably the worst journey for me as I was paranoid about the driver after catching him asleep at the wheel while driving. I saw his head just drop and he slumped, so I jumped up and grabbed the wheel. I could not settle after that. I kept looking in the mirror to see if his eyes were wide open. This really tested me – not being in control when I wanted to be. This same driver hit a large rock in the middle of the road about an hour away from Dengke and burst two back tyres, so we had to get alternative transport while the bus was fixed. When we finally arrived in Dengke we saw that the old cinema had been demolished and the site cleared, but Doctor Wujin offered us some of his land on which to build our Friendship Centre, so I and John Owens went out and put a returnable deposit on two big tiles and used them as boards to design the Friendship Centre according to our needs, which was accommodation upstairs and a medical centre on the ground floor, where volunteer doctors could perform medical procedures and operations. Then, at the end of the week, we returned the tiles and got our money back.

2007

I flew to Schiphol from our local airport, to fly on to Chengdu. This was when I met Phil Martin, an electrician who was going to rewire the front gates of the newly built Friendship Centre. We discovered that when the building was being built, the Tibetan builders laid the cables inside the concrete, and somewhere the live wire was touching the reinforcing inside the structure, making the front gates live – as Mel found out when he touched them and got an electric shock. I loved working with Phil. We would bounce ideas off one another. We spent the first week working in the local hospital, putting in electric sockets and lights, and in the treatment rooms we fitted two hand basins with hot water so the doctors could wash their hands after each patient. One day, after digging trenches along the back wall to a soakaway for the dirty water from the sinks in the hospital, a Tibetan man rushed up to me shouting something I did not at first understand. I worked out that he wanted a doctor for his friend, then his mates carried the patient in and laid him on a stretcher in one of the treatment rooms. I can remember seeing about eight men standing around, watching the doctor try to stop the bleeding before he was taken to a bigger hospital. The next morning there was a dog licking the blood off the floor. Sometimes we would see pigs walking through the corridor of the hospital! After a day's work we would head back to the Friendship Centre, have a meal, then Phil and I headed over the road to a teahouse for a beer. We talked for hours. I would tell Phil about my life and shared with him my faith in God, and he did the same for me. He encouraged me so much in my faith, and

I know I encouraged him. Sharing what God has done for you in your life with others is so powerful. I could see God revealing himself to Phil as we spoke; and, as Phil shared the things that troubled him, God showed him the answers.

During the second week at Dengke, we focused on getting the centre rewired, which we did – all but the upstairs lights. That week, we focused on putting partitions in the toilets. A couple of evenings, Marianne (a lab technician from Switzerland who was living in the Centre and working in the hospital) could not get a helper and she asked me if I could assist her with dressing some wounds on Shintso (a leper lady who had captured the hearts of the team who travel to Dengke regularly). I could not believe the size of the open sores on her knees, and she felt no pain as leprosy damages the nerves. Marianne cleaned the wound and poured honey over it, then put on a fresh dressing. She repeated this task twice a day for months until the patient was well enough to go back to her cave. Shintso got leprosy at a young age, but by the time she got treatment for it she was left with the severe disabilities that it had caused. The team used to visit her in her cave in a field outside the next village upstream along the Yangtze River. She kept calling me "honey, honey" while Marianne was dressing her wound, and I will never forget the childish giggle when Marianne explained to her in Tibetan that in English you would call your boyfriend honey! Once or twice a week we would pick her up, put her in a wheelchair and bring her to the Centre for tea. One day, Val and I made Shintso a bogey to sit on, with freely moving wheels, which had glove-like pads made of motorbike tyres to go over her hands to protect them so she could move herself along. She tried it out at the Centre and was so overwhelmed with it that she cried and kept holding on to us. I get a lump in my throat when I think of that time. Of anyone I have ever met, Shintso touched my heart, as she did that of every team member.

2010

Every year, when we arrive, one of the first jobs for me is to get the water on and the toilets working. I usually have to replace the flexi hoses and tap connectors as the cold damages them. So we put the water on, and on the first day I chase around, mending leaks and mopping up floods. We had the task of building a central heating system, using solar tubes on the roof, as the sun's rays are much stronger because of the high altitude (3500 metres). A multi-fuel burner and electric immersion were also piped up to the same heat exchanger, and because it gets so cold during winter (average temperature -10°C) we had to use anti-freeze solution in the system to prevent the pipes from bursting with the frost. We fitted radiators in the bedrooms. Phil and I really got the best out of each other by working together. Neither of us had ever done anything like this before, but we got it to work. We had some challenges, to say the least though. Because we were using solder copper pipework, we needed a gas blow lamp. The best we could get were small blow lamps like you would use to brown up food. So I came up with the idea of taping two of them together, with the flames merging. Then we could get the pipe hot enough to weld. Also, we found that the threads on the compression fittings were so small that as soon as you tried to tighten them up they just cross treaded, so we ended up having to solder them too.

It was not just work every day, we had Sunday as a day of rest. On one of the Sundays, Phil and I went for a walk up to the top of the mountain at the back of the Centre. It did not look that high until we started getting higher and the air was getting thinner, which made it even harder to climb what I thought was going to be a couple of hours' walk. It ended up being eight hours. But it was worth all the effort to see the mountains around, and Dengke so small in the valley bottom. We also had the pleasure of visiting Udren, the Tibetan girl in the book *Nearest the Sun*, and her family, on their traditional farm. I spent the best part of each day fixing burst pipes and building things, but I started feeling that I wanted to get out more and meet people and I began thinking: I am just fixing a building, and it is the people that need to know about Jesus. The building was very important because it is a base for us to go out to there, but my heart was changing.

2011

We travelled to Dengke in May on a big yellow bus, which was a real adventure, travelling along the very bad roads. In Dengke we had the task of running a waste water pipe from our building, through the next door neighbour's land, along a narrow dirt track and into a ditch on the other side of the main road. This was great as we hired labourers to help with the digging (mostly women), and a huge digger. We welded about 140 metres of 8-inch pipe and laid it out in the trench with a slight fall so the water would run along the pipe. Then some of the Tibetan guys who lived along the dirt track wanted to drop the middle of the pipe down outside their wall so it was deeper, making it fall backwards. I tried to explain that the pipe would fill up with silt and eventually block up if they had it running backwards, but they wouldn't have it. Anyway, the next year we came it was blocked! But it was so good to see our team working with the locals and sharing our cultures. I was talking one day to one of our Tibetan translators and he said: "It is great that you do these good things as it will earn you merits in your next life." This is what Tibetan Buddhism believes. This gave me the perfect opportunity to tell him about my belief, and that I am already saved and what we do is out of love because God loves us.

Another project was to build an incinerator to help get

rid of some of the waste. Also, we had been given a voltage regulator to help with the mains – a poor electricity supply was delivered to the building. I did not really know what I was doing but Phil Martin reckoned that I could install it. If only I had got the wires the right way round it would not have gone with a bang!

One day, we had a mother and daughter come to us in tears, asking if we could help the former's 22-year-old son "Nobo" who had been diagnosed with kidney failure. They had spent everything they had and borrowed money for medical treatment; they had nowhere else to turn for help. It was so heart-wrenching. Not being able to do something there and then, we put a message out to our local churches back home, and thanks to their generosity we were able to gift them with £2,000 to help him. Sadly, Nobo did not survive the journey to Lhasa for treatment, but we were able to pay off the mother's debts and medical bills.

2012

The practical tasks this year, included fitting partitions in the toilet block, laying a new drainage system, including a soakaway and building an outside loo (to use in winter when all the water pipes are frozen). We received a blessing, meeting up again with the mother (and her daughter) whose son had died of kidney failure the year before. When they came to see us they brought us a homemade gift of yak yoghurt. We have touched their lives by showing them God's love, and made true friends. Within our team we had two separate incidents of dog bites this year, thankfully not too serious. With the threat of rabies there was a window of only 24 hours in which to receive treatment, and the nearest place was two days' drive away. It seemed impossible. Solution: we arranged to collect the medication and brought the patient halfway, for us to meet the supplier, and everything turned out well!

2014

I remember this year because Mel became ill in Kangding and had to be taken back to Chengdu hospital while the rest of the team carried on up in the mountains. And when we arrived in Dengke, the mayor (Lubocho) said we could only stay two days, and that we should forget about the Centre as the government was going to possess it. So after some heated discussions with the mayor, and with the Chinese interpreters feeling very uneasy, we decided to leave town. But God was not finished with us on this trip so we went to help a kindergarten in Yue Xi by fitting a solar heater on the roof, to heat water, and provide hand washing facilities for the children and electric sockets in the classrooms. We also built retaining walls for planters and bricked up open windows in the toilets so as to provide privacy.

2016

This year, God proved his faithfulness by lifting all the oppression from us going to Dengke by removing the mayor and opening the doors to one of the monasteries where we went in and taught the young monks Bible songs and stories. The local police sergeant took a liking to us, and he and Mel hit it off with karaoke. Thanks to the police sergeant, four of us were able to cross the river into Tibet and climb up the mountain overlooking Dengke; then, walking down the mountain, we met two young girls collecting goji berries. We walked along with them to their village and they invited us into their home where we were able to bless the family and pray for their very elderly grandmother.

2017

Finally, I managed to get my wife Janet to make the trip to Dengke, with was a real highlight for me. Janet has been such a blessing by releasing me and supporting me for the many past trips over the years, by sacrificing: not having me around during some holidays, and times when she needed me to help at home. I would never have been able to do all I have done in Dengke without my lovely wife. Again, this was a year when we were free to visit Tibetan friends and teach in the monastery. The two girls from the Tibetan side of the river we had met the year before came looking for us when they heard that we (the foreigners) were back in town. Restrictions on foreigners were imposed in Tibet, but thanks to our friendly police sergeant we were able to visit the family and again pray for the elderly grandmother and bless them with new reading glasses, which poor people cannot get.

I look back over the years and I can see God's hand on the whole project. A small thing like introducing myself to Sue led to such a life-changing adventure of spiritual growth; meeting, and being part of, a fantastic team who share the same heart for seeing God's work in China and Tibet; how he has changed my heart and used my skills (for which I still don't feel like I'm qualified); doing the amazing practical things we have achieved. With God the Holy Spirit I have learnt that I can do anything. I have seen how God has changed the lives of many Chinese and Tibetan interpreters who have travelled with us – just by our being Christians and sharing God's love, the Holy Spirit breaks into people's hearts and reveals himself to them.

Chapter 9

NIGEL POOL
SUCH A PRIVILEGE

Nigel and I date back to the original hovercraft expeditions with Squadron Leader Mike Cole. Although he did not come on the actual "To the Source of the Yangtze" expedition in 1990, his total commitment and warm unparalleled generosity mark him out as a very special person. Always dependable, always prayerful, a brilliant "brother in the Lord"! What a joy for me when he was finally able to join us in the mountains and see for himself the terrain and people that melt our hearts. – Mel

My interest in China, and in particular the River Yangtze and its upper reaches, was kindled at a meeting at St. Peter's Parish Church in Farnborough, Hampshire, UK in the mid 1980s.

Mike Cole, a retired Squadron Leader, was speaking about a recent Joint Services Expedition to take a hovercraft to the challenging rivers of Nepal. The aim was to discover if it was possible to provide a Christian hover-doctor service to reach remote communities on the Kali Gandaki river.

The hovercraft was designed to operate in arduous conditions and to be repaired "in the field" – a concept created by Tim Longley who had been a Missionary Aviation Fellowship engineer in Chad where, due to the huge annual variation in the size of the lake, access to isolated communities at different times of the year was very restricted.

Mike gave a very interesting talk about the operation in Nepal, but he had a great vision for the future. Would it be possible to use this idea of "adventure with a purpose" to access the upper reaches of the Yangtze, to reach the source of this great river and, more importantly, gather together a group of gifted Christians with a wide range of skills to make a tangible difference to the communities along the way?

After the talk there was great interest, which was not surprising given that many in the audience were engineers and scientists from two of the largest local employers – the Royal Aircraft Establishment and the National Gas Turbine Establishment.

My own background was in heavy transport, diesel engines and hydraulic equipment, and I too had a moment to chat with Mike. As we were parting, Mike said, "I could do with your help; we have a team meeting planned, can you join us?"

And so I was hooked! Little did I realise how much I would become involved and just how much there was to do to get the Hovercraft Expedition to China ready for the launch in 1990.

Despite many technical, logistical and bureaucratic challenges, the Expedition travelled successfully to the upper reaches of the River Yangtze and one of the craft managed, despite ice and snow, to reach the navigable source at some 16,000 feet or 4800 metres above sea level on 11 June 1990. The record still stands today for the highest hovercraft journey in the world!

What was the legacy of this expedition? It was simply this: God used it to open a door in a very remote and sensitive, part of China, an area to which access would never normally be granted to Western travellers. When we are motivated by our Christian beliefs to go on an "adventure with a purpose" we can be sure that there will be more to it than we could ever imagine!

In subsequent years there were more hovercraft expeditions in other parts of the world and I continued to be involved behind the scenes in the UK. However, my interest in China remained and, as Mel Richardson and others returned to China on a regular basis, and Project Dengke became established, I kept in touch and helped where I could.

Then, at last, 25 years later in 2015, I had the opportunity to go to China, to travel to Dengke and to see for myself the people and places about which I had heard so much. With some trepidation, on Tuesday 28 July, I boarded the plane at Heathrow, arriving at Chengdu after some ten hours and 5,170 miles of travel.

Chengdu (the "Hibiscus" town) is situated in the south-western province of Sichuan ("the Province of Abundance") and is (in terms of resident population) quite similar to London. As we drove from the airport I was amazed at the size of the buildings, the cars, the shops, and the bright lights – we could have been in any Western capital city. The Minshan Hotel was to be our base and inside it was similar to any large international hotel. But, as I looked across the road from its main entrance, I realised that directly opposite was the Jin Jiang Hotel. At that moment I remembered the very frustrating bureaucratic wrangles that had delayed the 1990 Hovercraft Expedition, causing many of the team to be holed up in the Jin Jiang for weeks. Suddenly, it felt like I had really arrived in China.

My particular role within the team was to be responsible for the building maintenance works at the Centre in Dengke, and also for purchasing all the necessary plumbing, electrical and other components we might need. This had to be done in Chengdu before we left as there were limited supplies available in Dengke. So it was that some of us, and Nate our interpreter, armed with a Screwfix catalogue with lots of pictures, set off in a taxi to several industrial estates to gather all that was needed. What a wonderful experience! We came across all sorts of suppliers selling a whole range of goods, some of which were very familiar and others completely new to our Western eyes. Eventually, we garnered all that was needed and stored it in our hotel bedrooms until we were ready to leave.

On Monday 4 August we left the hotel and started our long twelve-hour drive to Kangding. Nestled in valleys at the confluence of two rivers, Kangding is a border town, about 2,600 metres above sea level, and a traditional trading post (tea from China and wool from Tibet). It is a beautiful place marked by a clear contrast between twenty-first century China and traditional Tibetan culture – an intriguing mix of the old and the new; prayer wheels and temples stand alongside all the trappings of the Western world. The thought occurred to me: how often people who live at a high altitude around the world (Tibet, Nepal, South America, etc.) seem to delight in a wonderful array of deep, rich colours in their cultures – notably in their clothing and buildings.

We were now amongst the Khamba Tibetans and very much in an area of traditional Tibetan culture, although outside the Autonomous Region of Tibet. In relation to the Christian gospel the Tibetans are perhaps the least reached people group, with fewer than one thousand believers worldwide. This was my first encounter with Buddhism. We felt privileged indeed to be invited by the owner of the hostel where we were staying to use his personal family room for our team briefings. Everywhere we went we were greeted with smiles, and not a little curiosity. However, we were also conscious of the obvious police and how privileged we were to be there at all.

I recalled the stories my parents had told me of Geoffrey Bull and George Patterson. Both were Christian missionaries based in Kangding when the Chinese invaded Tibet in

1950. Geoffrey was captured, imprisoned and tortured and eventually released some years later, whilst George, a doctor, escaped over the Himalayas in appalling weather. The small Protestant church was closed when we went to have a look and is seldom open, but there is no doubt that God has unfinished business in this place.

We spent a few days preparing for the next stage of our journey, meeting and helping some of our local contacts and exploring some of the sights of interest in the town. Breakfast at the Zhilam hostel further up the hill was definitely something to look forward to each morning. Some of us climbed the hill behind the hostel to reach the alpine meadow at the top – I have never felt so exhausted! At 2,600 metres it is tough if you are not used to it.

Early on Monday 10th we set off for our next stop, Ganzi, about eleven hours away. Here my main task was to install a shower at the home of Rigar, our guide. Rigar's family home is a traditional Tibetan house constructed from solid timber, beautifully carved and painted, outside the town, next to the family's fields. Close to the house is a large temple, three sides of which are lined with prayer wheels, and the fourth is a stone wall. Stuffed into the cracks in the wall were prayers written on paper or printed on fabric – this reminded me so much of the prayers placed in the Western Wall in Jerusalem, Israel. Two temples of very different purpose and origin.

On our first morning at Ganzi I could hear the noise of a heavy machine at work and wondered what it might be. I soon discovered next to our hotel a blacksmith at work in an adjacent shopfront, forging agricultural implements. I have always been interested in all sorts of engineering, and to see this skilled man at work was fascinating. Wherever we went there was a huge variety of businesses jumbled together, so different from the UK where we segregate our different types of workplaces. The following morning we woke up to find the road outside lined with flowers. Apparently a wedding procession was coming this way later in the morning, and placing flowers along the route is a local custom.

Three days later we were back in the minibuses and on the road towards Dengke. It was unusual for me not to be driving, so on each of these journeys I had the luxury of gazing out of the window, watching the scenery change from lowland to highland and then to snow-capped mountains and vast plains where yaks could sometimes be seen. It is hard to find words to express the splendour of the landscape. How could anyone think that it all arrived by accident? No, every mile was testament to a divine Creator.

But I was conscious too of the fragility of this environment. New high altitude airports, a railway, many large urban complexes, a desire to remove the nomadic population into permanent accommodation, hydro-electric schemes, and many more interventions by man, are threatening this precious eco-system, and will accelerate the rapid melting of the icecap (known as the Third Pole) and create other irreversible changes.

The Chinese Government sponsored inward migration of many hundreds of thousands of Han Chinese people into Tibet and the surrounding areas of traditional Tibetan culture. This is intentional, and designed to diffuse their rich heritage, with the ultimate aim of destroying all resistance to the Chinese occupation of Tibet.

Mile after mile of dusty narrow twisting roads, blind hairpin bends and sheer drops, and then, suddenly on the top of a rise we were presented with a view of the River Yangtze right in front of us, and way in the distance the small town of Dengke.

What an emotional moment! There in front of me was the river and place about which I had heard and read so much over the previous twenty-five years. That great river, the third largest river in the world, already 1,000 miles long at that point, was winding its way gracefully through a wide valley, creating a much disputed border, with the Autonomous Region of Tibet on one side and the Province of Sichuan on the other. Way in the distance, the community of Dengke straddled the land between the river and the mountains – a town which had grown considerably over many years.

Once we arrived at the Project Dengke Centre, tasks were allocated, and an assessment of the condition of the building was made. As there had been a total power cut in the community for the past month and the incoming main fuse had been blown apart at some point, there was no option but to try and find our small petrol generator, which had been "borrowed". Eventually it was found, and after some repairs, it produced power reliably for the whole of our time at the Centre.

With the plumbing, too, there were many problems, but an outside tap provided all we needed, even though we did have to carry all our water up the stairs to the kitchen and toilets. For us, and the locals, clothes were washed "under the tap".

We noticed on our arrival that our movements were being monitored carefully from a nearby building. Throughout our journey from Chengdu, at each stop, our papers had been examined and we had been allowed to proceed – something which could not be taken for granted.

Project Dengke only exists today because Mel and the team have been motivated by their Christian faith to love the Tibetan people. That in itself is not enough. It is only by demonstrating that love reliably, consistently and practically that relationships have been forged and cultural divides crossed. It is not possible to "dip in and out of" a country or culture and make a long lasting impact, it is only by persisting, with the Lord's guidance and direction, that a tangible difference will be made. We may not see that change but surely one generation will, for nothing is wasted in the Lord's economy.

So it is that the work achieved today is often the outcome of relationships built yesterday. This was particularly true of our relationships with local people years ago, many of whom are now in significant positions of authority. Shortly after our arrival, one of these contacts, a very senior official, made a considerable journey, unannounced, to visit us, and confirmed to those in authority locally, "These people are my friends." Certainly, the Lord had gone before us and was clearing any obstacles in our way.

Shopping for food and other items, exploring the town and its surroundings, eating in local restaurants, or even just watching the community at work and play, provided a wonderful insight into the lives of these Tibetan people. Raw meat was laid out on the pavement ready for you to choose from all the various components of a yak, while the butcher lazily waved a fly swat in the form of a yak tail. A solar kettle on the pavement – what an incredibly simple idea! They too wondered about these strange Western travellers, even though some of them were old friends of the Project.

Today everyone rides around on motorbikes, little tractors and other vehicles. I often wished I could have experienced Dengke in the early 1990s when horses were the primary form of transport and the town was so much smaller, untainted by petrol engines and Westernised products.

Very wet and overcast weather was brightened on two memorable occasions. The first was the opportunity to stand on the edge of the river on the site of Base Camp 1 of the Hovercraft Expedition – the main expedition base for the push towards the source of the River Yangtze. It is one thing to look at photographs and films but quite another to stand on the ground and recall all those stories.

The second very special occasion was an opportunity to

meet Udren, who in 1990 was the little girl who had stolen the hearts of the team members, particularly with the gift of her only toy "for the children in England". Now married with three children she stood with us in the rain with her husband and her youngest child. Dressed in traditional Tibetan costume (with pink crocs) she was clearly delighted to renew friendships with old team members and new – such a precious moment.

Around the perimeter of the Base Camp site and alongside the river there were many stones carved with Tibetan symbols and words. Indeed, wherever you go in Tibetan lands there are carved stones, prayer flags, prayer wheels, shrines and temples – for Buddhism and the Tibetan way of life are closely entwined within the culture of every community and family. So often in the West we regard Buddhism as harmless escapism in the form of meditation, yoga and simple living. However, I soon came to recognise that Tibetan Buddhism is a combination of the pre-Buddhist Bon animist religion and Buddhism that came over the Himalayas from northern India. It is a folk religion of rituals, which enslaves its adherents and consigns them to a life of fear, seeking to achieve impossible goals. Instead of mystical peace and harmony (John Lennon and Hare Krishna) the temples are full of demonic images and ritualistic homage. All of which is the complete opposite of the Christian faith, wherein God loves each individual sacrificially, our own efforts are useless in terms of them bring sufficient to "earn" salvation, and we gain redemption through his grace alone.

Despite our very different spiritual customs, it was always fun and a pleasure to meet local people. One such occasion occurred when Glyn and I went for a walk towards the eastern end of the town. Down near the river, where a small stream tumbled down the mountain to join it, we came across the barley miller. Inevitably he came to be called "Dusty".

His mill of mud walls and timber and grass roof straddled a mill stream created by diverting part of the larger adjacent stream. Each day when there was sufficient flow he milled barley to create "tsampa" – a staple of the local diet. He had no electricity, just an oil lamp. He was sitting outside the entrance to the mill as we arrived and, as neither of us could speak the other's language, we communicated by signs and gestures. Dusty pointed to my glasses and clearly indicated that he needed some – sadly my emergency pair was still at the Centre. Fortunately, a few days later, on the way home we had the opportunity to meet up with some friends going the other way, and in due course they delivered the glasses to Dusty – thank you Lord!

Soon our time at Dengke was over and we started the long journey back towards Chengdu. As I gazed out of the minibus window I saw a Buddhist monk on a pilgrimage, crawling along the side of the road, his hands bandaged but with blood clearly seeping through the bandages. I never noticed it at the time, but when I looked at the photograph later there was above him clearly the outline of a cross. I don't know what caused it, but to me, it is a visible sign of God's ever present love for those who are lost.

As we came within twenty or so miles of Kangding, one of our minibuses broke down on the hairpin bend of a steep mountain pass. Thankfully, the other minibus was able to operate a shuttle service back to the hostel, and a local mechanic was found to repair the bus, ready for our onward journey the following day.

I did notice the vultures circling overhead while we were stranded! I am not sure Western tourists would be very digestible. Truthfully, I was much more interested in the trucks struggling up the very long and steep pass, and the steam billowing from the hot brakes of those going down. Today most of these Chinese trucks are based on European technology, but you never see water used to cool brakes in Europe. Perhaps we might if we were to grossly overload them too.

Back in Chengdu we attended two special meals. The first was at the top of the Sichuan TV Tower, hosted by a long-standing friend of the Project. The tower is 339 metres high and has a revolving restaurant on the top, which gives incredible views of the city below. Then, just before we left China, we had a meal together with the Rinpoche. He is the local leader of the Buddhist community in the Dengke area, the most senior monk. He and Mel have developed a strong personal relationship, and it was a very happy and hugely encouraging note on which to end my time in China.

As I reflect on my personal journey with Project Dengke both here in the UK and in China I feel immensely privileged to have been part of such a godly team. I recognise just how much I need to learn, with God's grace.

Chapter 10

SANDRA WATSON
PRECIOUS MEMORIES

Sandra is one of those delightful ladies who always seem gracious, immaculate and smart wherever they are – be it up a mountain or in a "posh" restaurant. She has such a warm heart, a practical loving faith and thoughtfulness for those all around her. – Mel

As part of Project Dengke in 1992 and 1995, one memory that challenged and changed my perspective was the day I left the hostel to help build the bridge and found Shinsu the leper lady collapsed by the gate.

With only one foot and one thumb left, she had crawled for four hours from her hovel to get to the hospital. The final stretch was an uphill track from the hostel, for which she needed help. My initial reaction was a mixture of fear and concern that she might break if I touched her, but as a follower of Jesus Christ, his Spirit reminded me that Jesus touched lepers, so despite some locals expressing their worry for my health by calling out, she was scooped up and together we started the climb.

Half of the way there she needed to rest and I took the bottle of water and cup from my backpack and poured some out for her, but she would not drink from my cup. Instead she fumbled in her rags and produced a cracked bowl into which the water was poured.

My reaction was: please drink from my cup. But such was

101

her humility, plus a lifetime of separateness, that it brought tears from me even as she joined me in weeping.

We were the same age, and if she had been born in the UK she would have been whole and well, and if I had been born in her home I would have been the leper. It is so good to have the opportunity of putting oneself into another's shoes.

She taught me a huge lesson that day which has left me with the lifetime privilege of sharing an hour with the bravest woman I had ever met.

Chapter 11

SUE WERNHAM
I KNOW A MAN WHO CAN

Paul and Sue Wernham are what you might call the "the salt of the earth". They have worked unstintingly for many years for JHF (Jian Hua Foundation), seeking to send Christian professionals to China to help the country's development. Their love and dedication is unparalleled. It is not surprising, therefore, to see they had a major hand in getting John Glasby into our team – and what an incredible asset he has been. – Mel

It was at a "Salt and Light" residential mission weekend (involving a stream of churches we are part of) that one of those "God instances, not coincidences" occurred.

I went with a view to promoting China and JHF, should the opportunity arise. Essentially and typically, we target those with academic qualifications in education and medicine.

When someone with a good heart, a call on their lives and practical trade skills approaches us, it can be difficult to explain that we cannot help them. John did exactly this at that weekend, having been inspired to go on mission!

"Can you use a builder?" asked John.

"No, sorry, JHF can't" was the answer, "but I know a man who can."

Having Mel on our Charity Board meant that I was up to speed on his plans for his Friendship Centre and his need for quality tradesmen.

The rest is history, and my claim to fame is knowing the builder who handled the first brick.

Chapter 12

TAMAR
OH NO, YOU NEVER LET GO

Tamar (not her real name) is one of those special people with a very enquiring and sharp mind. She always likes to think through everything carefully before accepting any ideas. Eventually, of course, it is the Holy Spirit who convicts our hearts, not detailed arguments, and so it was with dear Tamar.

What a joy, some time after her conversion, that we were able to take her to a Matt Redman Concert in the UK to hear and see the man who wrote the inspired worship song that means such a lot to her. – Mel

"Oh no, you never let go, through the calm and through the storm, oh no, you never let go, in every high and every low, oh no, you never let go, Lord you never let go of me...." This was the first worship song that touched my heart on my first journey to the mountain. I remember we were sitting in the house of our Yi friends, worshipping our heavenly Father. And as an unbeliever back then in 2013 I had no idea about what this "fellowship" meant – I was just enjoying friendship with these lovely people whom I was trying to understand. Then David started to play this song with a guitar in his hands, slowly and softly, and it immediately gripped my heart.

"Even though I walk through the valley of the shadow of death, your perfect love is casting out fear...." The voice was low but the sound was firm. I was carried away by the pure joy and beauty.

I am a Chinese person who had been striving to be good and moral by our cultural standards. I came with the team as an interpreter because I was interested in Tibetan culture. I thought: I have a heart for this group of people. But when I was seized by anger and a sense of injustice when encountering the rude behaviour of an angry Tibetan woman on my second trip to the mountain in 2015, my belief in morality did not help in controlling my temper. Yet, strangely enough, I was immediately calmed by the words from my fellow brothers who were with me, experiencing the same unjust situation, and till today those words keep coming back to me at various times: "God has blessed us with so much grace and love that we don't deserve, so we should try doing the same to the people here."

At that particular moment I thought it made sense and I was convinced that we should learn to forgive as moral persons. But I did not think more about why we do not deserve God's love until we were back in Chengdu at the end of the journey. It was that night, I believe, that God opened my eyes to the truth of our Original Sin, and from whence he started to break the cultural bind on me, bit by bit. There has to be one God the Creator and the Saviour who blesses us by teaching us good from evil.

"Seek ye first the kingdom of God, and his righteousness, and all these things shall be added unto you, Allelu-Alleluia!" That night a few of us were singing this worship song in the hotel in Chengdu… "Seek and knock, and the door shall be opened."

Three years have passed since that rosy and enlightened moment, and this journey has not been without struggles and questions. God has made us in many different ways, and we may at times find ourselves struggling with interpersonal relationships, and we fall short of his glory. But praise the Lord, he has been constantly reminding me of his presence through his words, by guiding my work and sending many angels to my life wherever I go.

More and more is revealed as we follow him in spirit and in truth, I believe, while running on the path of faith with brothers and sisters.

Chapter 13

GLYN DAVIES
GOD INSTANCES NOT COINCIDENCES

My buddy Glyn is without doubt one of our most long-standing, faithful and wonderful team members. He took over the mantle of being my deputy after John Whatmore got involved in a great work in Uganda. His forte is administration and we sorely miss him when he cannot make it to the mountains with us. An avidly proud Welshman, his only fault is he hates karaoke, but never mind, we will get him converted one day!

Joking apart – this, his story, is a wonderful testament to God's grace. – Mel

I thought to myself: "What am I letting myself in for?" as I drove a minibus, with a bunch of friends, from Swansea to Loughborough in the spring of 1998. We were on our way to meet and listen to the committed Christian adventurer, karaoke-loving, "completely crackers" professor and inspirational leader who is Mel Richardson.

During the past twenty or so years that I have known Mel, I have had the privilege of being a part of Project Dengke. We have had highs, lows, very tough times, laughs, frustrations, weddings, and the most wonderful "God incidence" experiences, including the honour of being Mel's best man at his wedding to Ci Ci. Together we have been able to put into practice our motto: One person cannot change the world but we can change the world for one person.

There is a very special verse in the Bible: Ephesians 2:4,

"But God is so rich in mercy, and he loved us so much...."

"BUT GOD" . . . these two words which meant so much to my mother during her lifetime, have been important to me too during my remarkable journey with Project Dengke (PD). I have now been involved with PD for over twenty years, which includes over twenty-five trips of adventure to China, most of them ending up in Dengke.

I want to share the following stories that have brought me to tears, made me laugh, made me become angry and frustrated, but also have encouraged and challenged me. I have watched how God has intervened and provided, but at the same time I have learnt a lot of lessons. These lessons I hope can be of use to you, the reader, as well.

Being involved has meant I have met the most amazing people, and have seen and experienced God's incredible creation. Examples include: those wonderful rainbows which cover Dengke; the scene of the River Yangtze as it meanders along the valley, passing the town; the glorious vista of the range of mountains near Managanga; the glacial Green Dragon lake; the height of the Dengke pass (over 5,000 metres). We have experienced earthquakes, encountered and experienced tragedy, lost loved ones and friends, but also made lifelong friends. In recent years I have had the most amazing experiences facilitated by engineering. What used to take us twenty-four hours to get from Chengdu to Kangding City was reduced to twelve hours, and on our last trip took us only four hours on a beautifully constructed dual carriageway going through some 50 kilometres of tunnels.

My background is that I am a missionary kid. My folks were missionaries in the Congo (Belgian Congo as it was then) where I was born in 1952, and I lived there until 1960 when we had to leave the country in a convoy for our safety. We settled in Swansea, south Wales, where I went to school.

I served a six-year apprenticeship in printing and then

went on to work in several firms until I faced redundancy at the *South Wales Evening Post*, in Swansea. During the summers my Dad would speak at a conference in Kilcreggan in Scotland. Little did I know that Mel and his brother Keith used to take youth groups to this conference. During one of those sessions, Mel and Keith were challenged to "get involved" with overseas "adventures". Then, years later, our paths were to cross again. My Project Dengke adventure had begun. In the book *Nearest the Sun – The Story of Project Dengke* (2002), I shared my impressions and the lessons I learned from that very first trip. The adventure has continued. Back in 1999, I was given a love for Dengke and its people. I remember one very special occasion in 2019 when we were invited to attend the wedding of Rensa, Doctor Wujin's son. Tibetan weddings are full of colour, costume and culture.

I must say at this point that without the love and encouragement of my wife Ninon and our three children, Craig, Ruth and Claire, plus my Mum and Dad (David and Anne Davies) and the support of my home churches (Parklands and Woodlands) and the many who have supported us over the years, this adventure would soon have stopped.

During my early days in Wales my job with the newspaper had been a very good, well paid one. Then redundancy came. It is only when we look back that we can see how God was planning all of this. It was not easy at the time, as we often wondered where the next penny would come from. The redundancy money soon began to disappear as I was out of work for quite a long while. Had we not had job redundancy, I doubt very much whether I would ever have travelled to China, let alone over twenty-five times! Eventually, I was taken on as an administrator for Parklands Church, which effectively "freed" me up to be able to go to China. God knew our circumstances. He had plans for us. But it was not going to be easy. Being away from family for three or four weeks at a time, and working out how to pay for the trip, were huge concerns.

"BUT GOD...."
Unknown to us, God had "friends" lined up who would send us money for the trips. Some would post one-off gifts, others became regular supporters. Thank you to God and to every one of you for your love and support over these years. God supplied our every need.

One Christmas time we had a food hamper delivered to our back door. We still don't know where it came from – but it arrived just when we needed the food for our family.

Another time was when I took my two girls, Ruth and Claire, to north Wales. Ruth was attending the WEC summer youth camp and Claire had come along for the ride. We left Ruth at the camp and we then looked for an overnight stop. We found a B&B, but when it came time to pay the bill the following morning the owner simply said that an "angel" had already paid it.

And so it has been for the trips to China – God has been able to supply the necessary funds to pay for the flights, visas, accommodation and fees. On top of that, I have been upgraded several times on flights.

"BUT GOD...."
Out of the many journeys on which I/we have tried to reach Dengke, maybe at least three times we have been unable to get there. On one occasion we were the first Western tourists to arrive in Kangding and then we were turned around. During this time were able to find and meet new friends who are like-minded and love the area. A "God instance".

On another trip we only got as far as Shiqu (only sixty

miles away) and we were turned around! We spent a few days in Kangding, helping a family who needed their lounge redecorated. Later that same trip, we ended up going to Yuexi and blessing a local family who were planning to start a school in a few months' time. We were able to replace windows, rewire and paint the buildings, plus build a toilet block – another "God instance". It was on that same journey that David Vernon had the most amazing birthday celebration. Our host family roasted a pig in David's honour, inviting the whole school and the surrounding neighbours to the feast, which included cultural celebrations.

On yet another trip, when Mel could not be with us, we broke down about an hour's journey from Dengke. Both vehicles had punctures but we had run out of spare tyres. After ferrying the team and billeting them in the only local hostel, we were asked to meet with the local officials. These meetings repeated themselves daily for a week. We were unable to do much as the officials were still waiting for "permission to continue" for us. In the meantime, we prayed, enjoyed the local scenery and culture and made new friends. Although we did not do any practical work or teaching that week, we firmly believe that God was in control and that he had plans for us to pray for the town and its people. Several years later, we have seen the fruits of our prayers as permissions have been granted and relationships have blossomed.

"BUT GOD...."

A few years ago we almost lost one of our team members to the "Baskerville Hounds of Dengke". Pete Booth went down to the bridge which crosses the Yangtze into the Tibet Autonomous Region, to take a photo. As he edged next to the police checkpoint to get a good picture in this almost deserted part of the town, he was suddenly set upon by up to ten ferocious dogs of varying shapes and sizes, all seeming to want a piece of him. To say he was a wee bit scared would be an understatement. The fact that he had decided not to get the rabies jab before leaving the UK popped into his mind. Picking up a large stone, which under the circumstances seemed very light, he scaled a mud wall. It didn't seem tall enough and he was surrounded. Waving the stone he then quickly proceeded to make his way back in the direction of town, trying not to fall off this precarious wall which was barely six inches wide and which fell away at his feet. Thankfully, he got back all right, camera intact.

I also once had an investigative bite from an unfriendly hound near the monastery at the bottom of the hill. Thankfully, this was not serious but I learned to give wild dogs a wide berth.

More seriously, on another occasion I received a phone call at around 4.00 p.m. with the message: "Carey is down near the river bridge and has been bitten by a dog." Doctor Paul Harvey and I found him surrounded by several young monks, barely able to walk back to base. He was quite shaken up as he was bitten from behind and then fell over with the shock and severity of the bite. The big tooth mark prompted us into action. Paul treated Carey while our drivers went out to buy alcohol to dress the wound. We called Doctor Ray Pinniger for advice and began trying to contact the insurance company. But we needed Skype and the Internet.

We quickly asked Phil Martin to restore the electricity. He had installed a voltage regulator, but as we were just about to send out an email to the insurance company the electricity started to fluctuate as the voltage was too low for the regulator to work properly. We asked Phil to restore us to "normal" electricity, so at least we could send out the email. He succeeded, which was a blessing as we needed that emergency external contact.

Finally, we ascertained that Ganzi was the best place to obtain a further rabies jab capsule, and after calls to Rigar he helped us purchase the injection materials. Paul and Carey were dispatched without delay, soon after morning devotions led by Carey himself. All things ultimately worked out well. Rigar bought the injection, froze it and kept it safe and Doctor Wujin found us a driver. Carey was restored to us later. Ironically, that same week, one of the two newlyweds, John Owens, was also bitten by a dog as he was walking down the middle of the street. Despite not having had a rabies jab he survived that attack. More recently, we have learnt that all dogs have been removed, following horror stories that little children had been mauled and killed.

"BUT GOD…."

On one occasion we were side-tracked when the former town mayor arrived to seek advice on how to get his video camcorder to work, as his discs would not operate. Hannah, our resident tech expert, managed to establish that he needed to format the discs. Interpreter Bhamo then spent some time translating appropriate instructions. Meanwhile, he rang his son in the US who had purchased the camcorder and he asked if we had Skype.

What followed was very precious. We called the town mayor's lovely wife and she eventually came, as she lived some way away from the Centre. I set up a loudspeaker, and having got the son on Skype we left them together in tears. They had not seen each other for about seven years. What a privilege to serve in this way. We also hear that they are selling their home and moving into the town. They have also adopted six other children.

'BUT GOD....'

Several of our interpreters have become Christians, which is a great joy, and their stories are in other chapters. When people ask me, "Why do you continue sharing the gospel with your Buddhist friends?" I can do no better than refer them to this video:

https://youtu.be/5S9ABnRvqDk

Chapter 14

FIONA BLACK
NO ONE CARES ABOUT TIBET

I always remember being invited to Fiona's (or maybe her friend's) church to speak. It is the only C of E Worship Centre I have ever been to with armchairs in the front row. I thought to myself: how unusual, but how civilised! Like Fiona, I cannot remember how we first became acquainted. All I know is I am so glad we had such a talented person on our team at that time. – Mel

I was walking along the road with a friend, half listening to her talk about all the injustices of the modern world, until I heard her say: "And nobody cares about Tibet."

That stopped me. "Yes they do." I said.

She carried on walking. "Nobody ever talks about Tibet or pays any attention to it," she continued.

I hurriedly caught up with her, "Yes," I said again, "I know people who care", adding with faux-modesty, "I've been to Tibet", and I started to tell her about my trip to Tibet with Project Dengke.

To give you the context for this trip let me tell you a little about myself. I have earned my living in drama all my life, whether in theatre, film or television. I started as an actress and ended up behind the scenes managing productions. Coming from the north of Scotland I had little prior knowledge of drama but loved storytelling. Initially I went to drama college in Glasgow and, because I wasn't sure of the next step, studied for a Master of Fine Arts degree in the United States. Slowly I learned that there were many jobs and aspects to the business I had chosen, and throughout my career I had the pleasure of working in many different areas: as a Location Manager on *Darling Buds of May,* as a Stage Manager on *Bit of a Do* and Production Manager on many of the long running series, including *Holby City*, *The Bill* and *Eastenders*. I ended up producing *Waterloo Road* and latterly Line Produced on *Father Brown* in the Cotswolds, both marvellous experiences and great fun.

The nature of my work is peripatetic and I had to go where the work was, which could be anywhere in Britain. Also this was contract work and I often had gaps in between employment, so sometimes took these opportunities to do voluntary work. In March 2010 I was working for the BBC on the programme *Casualty*, and my contract had a couple of months to run when I received an email from Mel Richardson about Project Dengke. I am still not sure how or where I first heard about it, but Mel has been faithful in sending emails. I was not that faithful in keeping up with the news, but this time I thought that the dates worked and decided to go. I have to stress that I had no relevant experience, nor had I ever visited the East, but despite that I volunteered. There are hoops to jump through to visit China, including visas, the expense, and the time out of one's everyday life, so I had a few nerves about taking the step, but with the guidance of Glyn and the encouragement of Mel, who came and spoke to my small local church, I bought a rucksack and was ready to go.

If you have seen Ridley Scott's *Blade Runner,* the original of which came out in 1982, and if you can remember the effect of being transported to that futuristic cityscape, a world full of noise and contrasts, vast skyscrapers beside pails of pigs' heads, you will understand what it was like being in a

Chinese city for the first time. Just crossing the road was a wonder – there must have been hundreds of people at each side of half a mile of asphalt with twenty lanes jammed with vehicles waiting to crash down on you, and thousands of bicycles slipping and sliding round the edges. I might exaggerate but the traffic in China amazed me, and more so when I saw the vehicle which was going to carry us for 800 miles up to the roof of the world; basically we were going to travel in the Chinese equivalent of a very old VW van.

The journey was slow, and in parts there were no reasonable roads. We had to build pathways out of rocks to travel over streams. At other times there were vast tracks of concrete, built, so rumour has it, wide enough to carry tanks if required. It is good that the journey took days as it allowed the body to acclimatise to the altitude, and the brain to appreciate the changes from busyness to isolation, from city air to silent snow falling amidst prayer flags dancing above bottomless ravines. Tibet is a country which for centuries was closed to the outside world, later bartered as a prize between stronger powers; even today, no country in the world recognises the independence of Tibet. It is considered Chinese territory, yet Tibetans demonstrate a rich culture which is strongly rooted in Tibetan Buddhism.

Tibetan Buddhism struck me as a ritualistic belief. Its followers circled temples endlessly, counted prayer beads and turned prayer wheels. Strangely to me, temples were full of gigantic masks of demons. There were anomalies, as there are everywhere. Richly gowned monks accepted alms from people living in poverty, then drove away on motorbikes. Buddhism believes in reincarnation and finds its supreme spiritual leader through a choice made by other leaders and the direction of the smoke at cremation. The people are devout, displaying pictures of the present Dalai Lama on every wall, although this practice is banned by the Chinese.

Buddhism doesn't believe in killing, which might account for people self-immolating as a protest against the Chinese presence, rather than using more direct conflict. This belief system has held sway for many centuries in this, the highest region of the world. I was told by a young, female university graduate that to be a Tibetan is to be a Buddhist – that they are inseparable identities.

When we eventually arrived in the village of Dengke, high in the Himalayas, I could see that the Chinese had already made their mark. There is a Chinese fort and a large white school, the latter without electricity or water, desks or teachers, but it is a symbol of Chinese progression. We arrived at night in the pitch dark (there are no street lights) and immediately there was a visit from the Chinese police. Their message: we could stay but we must not interact with Tibetans. We could buy food and go for walks but must not integrate, have conversations or offer medical help. Since both teaching and medical aid were the aims of the journey it seemed we were stymied.

I suppose in a strange way this left me with access. As mentioned, I have no particular skills and so I tagged along with the professionals to help out organising meals and washing up – it was the best I could offer. We had bought food in Chengdu before leaving, and our first meal was spaghetti Bolognese.

To be clear, we were a mixed bag of Europeans, Tibetans and Chinese, and the latter included our two drivers, Mr Chen and Mr Lui. Very quickly after our first evening meal these drivers offered to help with cooking, they were not impressed with pasta. I still can't look a fish in the eye without thinking of them. Fish eyes, chicken heads, pigs feet were all employed. With one fish they would make a meal for twenty of us. Lots of little bowls and strange combinations, guts, bones, everything went in. The two drivers could cook:

lots of hot oil, lots of spices, using vicious looking cleavers to slice ingredients at high speed, the results were always delicious.

I still made breakfast or helped David Vernon, a veteran of the expedition, who did most of the work – he would make porridge, boil eggs and set the table while my job was to walk to the bakery and buy the bread. Getting the bread was not simple, it took all my courage. Towards the end of my time I asked others to go in place of me, or at least to come with me. To explain: getting that bread was like running a gauntlet. You see the Tibetans won't kill anything and there are gangs of dogs roaming the street. Now I like dogs but these dogs are wild and there is only one street in the village. The dogs are nocturnal and bark all night, (which is very irritating) but generally they slept during the day, so when shopping you could tiptoe through them or around them ("let sleeping dogs lie" and all that). But first thing in the morning, with no-one else around, the smell of fresh bread woke them and they would start to follow me, one or two at first then more gathered. These are not pretty dogs, they have matted fur, running sores; they growled and fought and would kill the weak or puppies. The Tibetans say that they all have bites on their bottoms from running away from them, and their advice was to throw stones at the dogs, which is kind of confusing. I suppose I wasn't meant to hit them but my arms were full of bread anyway so I couldn't. I dreaded those walks more and more but survived, unbitten, for five weeks. The Chinese used to shoot the dogs but the Tibetans objected, I have to say I tend to side with the Chinese over the dogs.

Of course it is obvious that Tibet is far removed from the country that I was accustomed to, but the weather, and in particular the dust storms, were a feature that amazed me. At four in the afternoon everything stopped, clothes were taken off the washing line, everyone disappeared inside and windows and doors were shut and jammed with paper or material to stop the dust creeping in. I am not sure of the reason for these storms, probably just the airflow at that altitude, but I had never imagined a dust storm in that rarefied atmosphere, and for me they added to the mystery of the region.

Another thing that amazed me, and this has to do with gender equality, is that women seem to do all the manual labour. On the road up the Himalayas any road works seemed to be completed by women in highly coloured embroidered clothing who operated picks and shovels with great professionalism. Later at Dengke when the team were hiring labourers to put down drainage pipes only females volunteered for the work. I am not sure if this proves that the Tibetans are highly emancipated or that so many of the men become monks which means that the women have to take over most of the other jobs.

One of my more exotic discoveries was Tibetan "gold" known as "worm grass". I was introduced to it when I was offered some dirty looking twigs when we visited the Green Dragon Lake. horrified by the look of them, I refused. Later it was explained to me that I was being offered a great delicacy. There is a fungus which eats the caterpillars of moths and is said to produce a substance which has medical value and is said to cure many ailments and is much in demand. I believe that you can make it into a sort of tea. I have never tried it but this fungus is harvested in the summer for its properties, and those who gather it sell it at a great profit in the city. I believe other regulars to Dengke have tried it and acknowledge that it has benefits.

Before going to Tibet I had heard about sky burials, the custom where human remains are left to be eaten by carrion birds, which to Western thinking seems extreme but is actually disposing of the body in as beneficial a way as possible. In the Himalayas the ground is too rocky for what is considered normal burial in the West, and because of the scarcity of fuel, there are few trees so it is a more practical solution than cremation. Although never having seen such a funeral I was told that the monks would "call" the birds by ringing a bell. These birds are mainly vultures. On one of our trips up the mountains we rounded a corner and a huge bird posed on a tree. It seemed unafraid of us and quite aware of its own beauty. This was a vulture, the first I had seen other than in photographs, and I was amazed at how majestic it was.

Perhaps the Tibetan habit which I found most astonishing and strangely appealing was walking backwards. I found out about walking backwards when I saw a couple slowly, but with confidence, walking backwards through the village. I had to find out why, and it was explained to me that this was a way of staying young. If you walked backwards you preserved your youth. Thinking about it, it doesn't seem any more silly than a facelift. I have looked it up since, and it appears that walking backwards has benefits. Researchers have found evidence that backward locomotion appears to be a very powerful trigger to mobilise cognitive resources, and there are many examples online. Seemingly, Eastern societies have long practised backward locomotion (also known as walking backwards), well aware that 100 steps backward walking is equivalent to 1,000 steps in conventional walking. It is also meant to make our five senses more alert.

Finally, in response to my friend, I have to admit that Tibet doesn't get much attention – not as much as it deserves for its unique character and its wonderful differences. Perhaps the most memorable aspect of this nearly forgotten land is the scenery: the Himalayas, with its deep ravines; the vast stretches of water, like Green Dragon Lake, which lies motionless and feels timeless, reflecting the mountains. This scenery, combined with the abundance of wild life, is all preserved by the fierce independence of its nomadic people. My friend's words that "No one cares about Tibet" remind me how much there is to care about in Tibet, which inhabits one of "the uttermost parts of the earth".

Reference
Hitti, M (2009) *Facing a Challenge? Backing Yourself out of it – Literally – May Help*. Koch, S. Psychological Science, May 2009; vol 20: pp 549-550. Online. Available at https://www.emedicinehealth.com/script/main/art.asp?articlekey=100160 Accessed 15th January 2019.

Chapter 15

GEOFF MARSHALL
I THINK WE HAVE BEEN MUGGED

Geoff (now in glory) was one of my special buddies. As described earlier, he was a key member of the "men in the shed" early morning prayer group that we both belonged to. Some say he was even more eccentric and crazy than I am. All I know is his knowledge of scripture and the recent history of the Royal Navy was astonishing. His hilarious stories of "goings on" on board submarines and ships kept us amused for many hours. His warm-hearted desire that all should hear the gospel, and be saved, was undoubted. Come rain or shine, sickness or health, outside my church (where he was an official morning service "welcomer") whenever he was asked "How are you?" he always replied "Rejoicing". Likewise, we could predict the afternoon weather from what he was wearing. If in shorts – sunshine. If in sou' wester, looking like a lifeboat man – rain.

Read on…smile….and enjoy!   – Mel

The urge to visit Dengke came from seeing photos shown at church by Mel – one image in particular depicting a man arc welding wearing sunglasses for his eye protection. I thought the least I could do was to take him a welding mask. That proved to be the easy bit. Getting to Dengke was more protracted. My passport was in date, so the next hurdle was getting a visa. To obtain a visa for China one must present oneself in person to the Chinese embassy in

Bond Street, London – otherwise known as the "Nightmare on Bond Street".

The doors opened at 9:00 am promptly and closed just as promptly at 10:00 am! I mention this because unless one wishes to visit the capital twice and incur more rail expenses you need to pay for an express visa which is £50, as opposed to a £30 one. Having obtained the visa, the flight booking is next. I was travelling from Southampton to Beijing. Beijing was where the fun began.

Travelling alone, and being the only European, was daunting. In among the hordes of people I spotted David Vernon, who I knew from a China Day at home. I think we were both relieved to see each other. We were discussing onward flights to Chengdu which we had not booked when two ladies came out of the crowd milling around us, pressed tickets into our hands and promptly disappeared. In what seemed like no more than two minutes, two more ladies, in crumpled uniforms, sidled up to us and asked us for our passports and tickets. They told us to follow them. We did this so that we could keep our passports in sight. We ended up outside the airport where we were asked for approximately $10 each. The money was handed over, we were conducted back into the airport to the front of the queue for the flight to Chengdu.

David remarked, "I think we have been mugged!" – and I didn't disagree. Landing at Chengdu we were met by people who seemed to know us but we didn't know them. Ultimately, we ended up at the hotel. We met Mel later, and we spent the next three days collecting cold weather kit and sleeping bags, and meeting all the rest of the team. On about the fourth day, early at 6.00 a.m., we all set off for Dengke in an eight-seater bus and a Pajero Jeep. This is where my work began.

Mel had a memorial tablet made out of marble. It was

dedicated to his late wife Jackie, and he had intended to stand this against the foundation of the Friendship Centre. We managed to slide it into the minibus through the back door, and to stop it from sliding we kept our feet on it.

It took us about four days to reach Dengke, which is in the Tibetan mountains, approximately 3,500 metres above sea level. Two incidents stand out, apart from altitude sickness. First, there was a sheet of ice covering several yards of road where the driver of the bus thought he would lose control and go over the edge, and what I suggested was to get everyone out of the bus and to get the Jeep across to the dry side of the road and thereafter use it to tow the bus across the ice, which is what we did, successfully. The second incident was when the Jeep kept stopping and I thought it might be fuel blockage. We got around this by bypassing the fuel filter using a length of catheter tube from the surgical kit of one of the doctors who were with us.

Another incident that happened to David and myself was the invasion of bed bugs at the hotel in Kangding. David was my room mate and we found that the sheets were a little damp. We turned them back and spontaneously all these little black fellows leapt out. We spent another thirty minutes despatching them.

On reaching Dengke we stayed at the house of Wujin, who was the local doctor. His mother, at the age of 85, used to get up early so that we could have hot water for shaving. I do remember being taken to the unfinished Centre in the company of Jeff Bird, another doctor, to work out where the surgery was going to be. He was describing to me what operating theatres were like in Australia, and I had a little knowledge of what size a theatre would be required, but seeing the proposed area in the Friendship Centre, doubts began to set in. We both told Mel, who roped in Wujin, who then said that he only wanted a dispensary.

Then came the moment for my reason for the trip. I presented the helmet and welding gloves to the lad I had seen in the photograph. He was very pleased with the helmet but when he tried to put the gloves on I found I had brought two right-handed gloves!

Comment from Mel: The Tibetan welder's incredulous look, first at the gloves and then at Geoff, was hilarious. You could almost see his brain thinking: "Is this a joke or what...?" Quite rightly, Geoff refused to wear the welding suit that had been provided for him and handmade in Chengdu when he found it to be made of inflammable nylon. We all decided that we didn't want Geoff to be turned into a human torch after all – "elf and safety rules, okay?".

Chapter 16

DC
HOW GREAT THE GOD WE SERVE

D, along with his wife R (otherwise known as "Rocket") are perfect companions to have on a team. Both are delightfully unconventional, warm-hearted, loyal and abounding in energy. D, in particular, if he sees a mountain has to climb it. Turn your back and he disappears, albeit for a short while. Great guys! – Mel

It seems to me that every person's life is eventful and fascinating, but I find it hard to discern which aspects of my own journey might be interesting to a reader. I apologise if any of the details I include seem unimportant or uninteresting – I can journal truthfully what I remember, but am less good at editing something to produce a coherent narrative which a person might enjoy reading; please bear with me!

I first heard about PD whilst sitting in the back of a bus in 2011, being driven back to Antananarivo from Antsirabe in Madagascar. After spending some time in a small village called Beroroha helping the locals there to put the roof back on their marketplace, our small team was returning home. During the long journey back, team leader Andy was asking people what their next steps would be. Andy knew that I had been to China many times by then, and that I had some connection with the People's Republic of China – either deliberate or accidental! He told me about Mel, and how a hovercraft which was being used in Madagascar to transport doctors (and water filters) to remote villages along the

Mangoky River was once part of a project to fly up a river in China. He suggested that I should get in touch with Mel to "push that door" and see what would happen.

At the time I was single, and had come to realise that my lack of attachments and relative physical health (as well as a taste for adventure) enabled me to sign up for some really risky things. I had also always had an interest in doing "charitable" work, or for volunteering to help others. I cannot say that it is my natural inclination to be selfless, so I can only assume that it was the Holy Spirit guiding me in this way. PD seemed both to offer a real tangible level of adventure and a unique opportunity to serve others for His glory in an interesting place. I felt that I was in a position to be able to offer my service to them in 2013, in a way that I would not have been able to had I had kids to look after, or a wife/girlfriend at home to mourn me! I also had no problem leaving all the familiar things of home for long periods of time; perhaps I even preferred it that way. Having been to China many times for leisure, I had a basic grasp of the spoken language, as well as an interest in the culture.

I got in touch with Mel, and we agreed to meet in London one day for coffee and a chat. I remember a bit about the chat – he told me about the project and its heart, and said I had been recommended by Andy (which surprised me!). Unfortunately, there is a gap in my memory between my London "interview" and the time I was standing with nervously sweaty palms in front of my then boss (at a bicycle distributor) asking him if I could take five weeks of holiday during peak season! I had prayerfully decided that I would be going on PD whether the boss agreed or not, so I was essentially finding out if I would still have a job to come back to. Thankfully, my manager was in the room with me and the director and the manager seemed to understand that I was not asking for permission to go, but rather asking whether I would need to fill in a holiday form or hand in my notice. Praise God that they decided to let me take the time off without issuing me a P45.

So, in the summer of 2013, I joined my first PD. En route, Heathrow delayed my luggage after being nervous about some spray deodorant that was in my checked bag. This might not sound like too much of a problem, but when you transfer to a domestic connection within China, you need to be there to collect your baggage at the first point of entry and take it through customs yourself. I arrived in Chengdu without my bag, which I suspect later arrived in Guangzhou with no one to collect it and take it through customs. Heathrow claimed to have sent it, Guangzhou claimed not to have received it, and so it has remained – forever lost. The only items I still had in my possession on arrival into China were my Bible, a pair of boots and the clothes that I was wearing. I had to sleep in the underwear I had worn on the flight and go shopping for new clothes the next morning. A word to the wise: always take a change of underpants in your hand luggage. Despite this initial setback, I quickly made friends on the team and found local friends to skateboard with in Chengdu. It was during this time that I met a cheerful young Scot who would remain my close friend for the rest of the project.

PD in 2013 was a frustration to many in the group who were disappointed to discover that we could not go to our intended destination, and therefore had to make other plans. To the disappointment of some newer, younger additions to the team (myself included), it was decided that we would go on "holiday" instead for a while. I was eager to get my hands dirty and was frustrated by what I saw as a distraction. Knowing me, I was probably not *quietly* disgruntled! I also argued that we should take the two Chinese drivers with us on "holiday" to Dege, despite their refusal to drive us there – which Mel interpreted as a breach of contract. I was afraid that I had spoken out of turn, but another team member encouraged me that others were quietly thinking the same.

The mountains were breathtakingly beautiful, and the roads (in the process of being fixed as we used them) were as rough as any I had experienced in Africa. The altitude had a habit of giving me a headache when we went hiking (quite often), and made cooking meat a challenge without a pressure cooker. Having lost my sleeping bag (did I pack one?) with my luggage, I had the privilege of sleeping under yak furs in Ganzi. As we got higher into the mountains and the temperature got lower, I bought warmer clothing, and enjoyed buying a sturdy knife in Kangding to make me (falsely!) bolder going for hikes in areas known to have bears and wolves. Did I think I could beat a bear with a knife? Perhaps not, but if forced to fight a bear, I would rather have had a knife than not! Packs of wild dogs kept the bears and wolves out of the towns for the most part anyhow, and their din in the night reminded us not to wander out after dark.

After the holiday (which was actually very fruitful) we changed course and headed to a village in the south to help members of a different minority group (the Yi) by renovating a house for use as a kindergarten for Yi children to help them "catch up" with their Han peers. This frustrated some of the other members of the team who were hoping to work with Tibetan people exclusively, though I and some of my teammates were excited finally to be able to do some practical stuff, and we had no preference regarding the ethnicity of those God had called us to serve. I felt puzzled that people seemed to be making a fuss about having to serve one minority instead of another but, in retrospect, it can be hard if you feel called to minister to one people group and you are placed in an area where that people group is not living. With hindsight I can relate, as I felt similar frustration thinking I should be living in China, when His plan was for me to live in the UK for 10 years. I like that Arthur Ashe quote: "Start where you are, use what you have, do what you can". I do believe that God gives people a heart for certain peoples or places (God Himself has a heart for all people, I believe), but that this love should never be made *exclusive* by our own designs; to avoid or refuse, based on our own preferences (or even calling?) to help certain people he puts in our path.

One event from 2013 which stands out for me is the roadside scuffle we witnessed. On the road to Manigange we came across a traffic jam caused by a huge truck (driven by Tibetans) getting stuck in mud in an area of the road which was being repaired. The Chinese construction worker who came in a digger to dig the truck out was being threatened by the two Tibetans (who were holding rocks). Our "mother figure" translator ("T") courageously stood between them and the digger driver and asked for peace, telling the Tibetans that threatening the construction worker was silly, as we could not fix the road without him, and telling the Chinese worker that we loved and valued him. After a little while, however, some other construction workers (about ten of them) who had heard that their friend and co-worker had been threatened drove down and threatened the Tibetans. The Tibetans picked up rocks again, at which the crowd of workers beat them up, using bits of metal rod, hammers and other tools. As they were starting to fight, I began walking towards the ruckus (inspired by T's actions) with a view to breaking it up. Our driver shouted at me and, shocked by his sharp tone, I obeyed his shouts to get back in the vehicle. A whole jam of vehicles full of people all looked on as ten people armed with construction tools beat up the two men. After it died down, some medical experts from our group went to help the man, who was then lying in his own blood (the larger of the two Tibetans seemed to have escaped mostly unharmed). I have regretted my decision to return to the bus, and it still bothers me today. The driver told me that "if an outsider sees two friends arguing and tries to interfere he can have his own arm broken" or something similar, but I think that healing a broken arm is easier than having to live with a cowardly decision.

The second "PD moment" from 2013 which stands out in my mind is when we were on the road to Dege "on holiday" in two bread vans. On a narrow road, the wing mirror of our van clipped the wing mirror of a van coming the other way, and naturally a discussion between the two drivers ensued. The only problem was that our vehicle did not have a working handbrake, and we were parked on an upward slope with a cliff-drop behind us. Sitting in the front passenger seat, I had to reach my foot across the central divide and jam my left foot on the brake pedal to keep us alive whilst the driver got out to chat with the driver of the other vehicle! There are many other stories from 2013, including various rumoured love interests, three people beginning their journey to faith, butchering and roasting a whole pig for a birthday party, passport troubles, Karaoke times and more, but perhaps they are other people's stories to tell.

Ever since my first time in China I had hoped that I would be able to live there, but I was frustratingly delayed for a decade. This all made sense, of course, when I met my now wife in England. Shortly after I returned from PD, I met her for the first time, at a friend's monthly young Christian event. She had decided that it would be her *last* attempt at attending a Christian event, and I was not planning to attend, but a mate I was supposed to meet for dinner that night had decided he would rather get drunk, freeing me up to go along. My (now) wife and I met washing dishes after the event, introduced by a mutual friend (who would

eventually give the sermon at our wedding one year later).
I was sweaty from skateboarding, my breath smelt of garlic
and chilli from the Sichuan soup I had had for dinner, and my
tattered clothes matched my non-matching shoes. It was a
miracle that she wanted to meet me again. At that time, I had
also just found out that I had been accepted for a six-month
project back in Madagascar, fixing the hovercraft there. My
wife and I started dating in December, and she visited me in
Madagascar during my time there. After we were reunited
in the UK, we went to China on holiday together, where we
were engaged, and were then married on our first anniversary.
During our tour of China in 2014, my then fiancée and I felt
that we were being steered/called (finally) towards China,
and were planning to use our time on PD to be open-heartedly
asking him where He was guiding us, and what to do. We
kept "honeymoon" as our excuse for joining PD together in
2015, though we had to move out of our house to join that
year (as property guardians we were not allowed to be away
from the property for more than two weeks). Somehow, my
old job was waiting for me after six months in Mada (they
offered me a job by email whilst I was still there), and I only
started work there providing they would allow me to join
PD again in the summer.

I was surprised that Mel was enthusiastic about having
me join PD again in 2015 after my making a nuisance of
myself on more than one occasion! That year the team was
delayed in Kangding for a week or so while Mel returned to
Chengdu to collect his passport. That time of "delay" was
great – we were able to make friends there, and to help a
group of friends to decorate their house. These friends also
owned a business which might have led to an opportunity
to live and work in a scarcely visited area of Sichuan, and
this prospect excited us. My wife celebrated her birthday in
Kangding, which we marked by eating a cake shaped like a

bear's head in a Tibetan restaurant.

That year we managed to make it all the way to our destination, where I thoroughly enjoyed cooking meals for the team, as well as making sure that the drinking and washing water was kept well stocked – a full-time job with a large team and only one working tap (outside, downstairs). The pipes had frozen and burst over the winter, so there was no running water in the building, and a rumoured dispute between the town and an electricity provider meant that the only power in the town was from petrol-run generators. During the trip, we were pleased to hear that the second of the three non-believing translators from 2013 had been baptised, and the third made a commitment. Those three really demonstrated that God uses many different means to draw his children to him – one of the girls was baptised very quickly, another's heart was softened by seeing a believer show compassion to a leper on PD 2014, the third became convinced after many long discussions, frank questions and honest answers. During the trip, my wife and I were coming to think that we might be called to spend our lives in the mountains. This was on our mind during our time in Dengke, as well as our short stints in Ganzi and Kangding.

It was on PD in 2015 that we made a friend under strangely "coincidental" circumstances. We had skateboarded with a Chinese guy the night before we left for Kangding – he and I had been trying the same trick for quite a while and encouraging one another. The next day, after a long drive (traffic jam as usual) to Kangding, we were invited to a bar hidden away down a side alley and over a shop, by a local Kangding skateboarder. On arrival at the bar, we met the same man from Chengdu we had been skating with the day before. It turned out that Kangding was his home town, and he had been driving down on the same day as us. To this day, we are good friends with both him and the owner of the bar, who have both since married and had children. We believe that our meeting in this way was no accident, but that it was engineered for a purpose which we may understand one day, in this life or the next.

The year 2015 saw me truly testing the team's patience again (I cringe to remember the event) when I went off for a 90-minute wander around a lake when everyone else had been ready to go home after 15 minutes. Having no working phone, and having gone by myself, the other team members were concerned for my safety, and after 45 minutes or so hired a man on a motorcycle to go searching for me. Oblivious to the drama unfolding back near the vehicles, I trundled my way around the lake, arriving back casually on the back of a horse I had managed to hire at a discount. As they saw me coming over the hill on the back of a pony, the team's concern turned to anger, as I had kept them all waiting for over an hour. I felt mortified to have caused so much grief, and ended up paying 100 RMB (if I remember correctly) to the motorcycle "rescue team" when they finally caught up with us. I felt certain that Mel would never invite me back on a team after that.

On arrival back in Chengdu, we shared with a PD veteran and friend about our opportunity to go into business in the mountains, expecting her to be encouraging about the prospect of living in that region (as many of the others on PD were). We were surprised that she suggested, instead, that we should help a group we had heard about in the UK who were working in orphanages in Hunan and Henan. To cut a long story short, our application to work for that charity was accepted, and I quit my job (again) and we moved to Henan to work with disabled children. We were told by the management of our new employer that we would not be allowed to join PD in 2016, but that we should be able to join in 2017 if we used our annual leave to do so.

During our time in Henan I found myself working in a bizarre environment, one where I felt a bigger culture clash with the international team than with the local Chinese teachers and therapists. It was a blessing to work with the lovely kids and wonderful, hard-working local staff. We quickly made friends in the community, and had a deliberate strategy of "putting down our roots", wanting to play the "long game" to enable us to stay there as long as possible without burning out, as this would be the best way to have a positive effect on the lives of the abandoned children we were there to help. It was the first time that I had worked in a female-dominated environment – my straight talking, outward-speaking tendencies often came across as being insensitive. I felt that the frictions were a natural part of working in a high-stress environment, and our relationships with the other team members became (at least functionally) better over time. Despite this, we never had any similar struggles working with the Chinese staff, who were both lovely and encouraging. I felt that I was a difficult person by nature, and I felt so convinced that I was more of a hindrance than a help that when Mel not only invited us to join his team as translators but also to pay for our flights to Chengdu, I almost cried. I had forgotten what it felt like to be valued as a member of a team, and Mel's invitation was a much needed encouragement. After twisting a few arms, we were allowed to take the time off. We arrived in Chengdu thanks to Mel, and enjoyed the Western breakfasts in a way only those who have lived overseas in a small town for more than a year can understand.

Mel's invitation to return to the team not only as members but as translators and for him to pay for our transport out of his own pocket was a truly gracious opportunity given to us despite my glaring flaws and mistakes (on both previous teams), and a huge blessing during a time when, despite putting my all into the work, I felt unwanted and discouraged.

It felt good to revisit friends and places on PD in 2017 which we had first seen as newlyweds. My wife celebrated her birthday in Dengke this time, and the cooking responsibilities were divided equally among team members, allowing me to join in the other activities (as well as having a good bash at getting to the top of some of the nearby hills during leisure time).

Something happened in the team that year which might seem like a negative thing, but I think it was ultimately positive and life-giving: I and one of the other members of the team had a pretty serious falling-out. I had woken up to do the breakfast shift to find that the oatmeal I had planned to cook for breakfast was open, and some of it had not only been used, but had been left on the side, glueing several bowls together in an untidy pile. At breakfast, I asked what had happened, and had expressed distaste for the waste of food and the mess in the morning. It turned out that some of the girls had opened it to use as exfoliating face treatment! Since we were living on handouts in a small town, my wife and I could rarely afford oatmeal. Another member of the team was quite cross with me for being critical and for embarrassing the girls in question, and we exchanged loud, short words over the breakfast table. Later on, I looked for her to have a chat and found her searching for me for the same reason. In an unoccupied bedroom, we both expressed our points of view; we learnt much about each other's situations and perspectives and, during the discussion we grew closer in community. After that we got on famously, and at the end of the team she even offered to pay for our rent for a year! I truly believe that disagreements need to be aired, communication kept open, and difficult discussions not avoided.

On arrival back in our "hometown", in Henan, we quickly

learnt that the project we were helping with was potentially closing down. At first I thought there was no way that it could really be closing down, as there seemed to be no major problems with the practical running of the project – not to mention the obvious positive effects of the charity's help on the well-being of the children. By about Christmas time (which I felt was an intensely demanding period) we found out that the project was actually quite likely to close down, and for reasons which I did not understand or agree with. So we spent our first Christmas away from home grieving for the project, grieving for the children's loss of support, and also despairing for our future; we would likely have to leave the town we now called home suddenly. With all the extra events and extra expenses, we were burnt out and did not really recover until Spring Festival break in February. Throughout we were also not allowed to share the uncertainty of the project's continuance with our supporters. We felt shaken, betrayed and stranded.

We expected that the charity would relocate us to a different project, and were getting used to the idea of living in Henan. We were told to expect to be moved to another project elsewhere in China; all should go smoothly, even though we would have to leave our home and the children that we had served and the local staff we had worked alongside (not to mention our friends in the community). We found out quite suddenly (it came as a shock to almost everyone) that we would not be invited to join another team. I felt that the reason we were rejected from the other project was due to my personality; that my character flaws outweighed the benefits that we could bring to a team.

My mother-in-law came to visit, and we had a pastoral visit from our true friend from that charity who had been encouraging throughout when it felt like everyone else was against us. We carried on at the Welfare Centre (orphanage), after the rest of the international team had left, for as long as our visas allowed us, but found out, after a long process of investigating every avenue, that getting a new work visa (a prerequisite for working in the Centre) would be impossible for us. We had to start investigating whether the next move would be to return to the UK, or go somewhere else in China. If China, where? To do what? During this time we had another encouraging message from an old friend (the one who had encouraged us to help the abandoned kids in 2015) whom I had met on PD in 2013. She said that she understood that our discovery that we needed to leave our home in Henan might be bad news for us, but that it might be good news for her: our skills could benefit her social enterprise in Chengdu. After the feeling that I was terminally difficult, and having our applications to relocate after more than two years of service rejected, we were touched to the heart by our friend's encouraging invitation. We were unsure of the viability of applying for a work visa, nor how we would move our stuff, but we made the decision to move to Chengdu and give it a shot.

Again, during a time of heartache and rejection, feeling that our best efforts were not good enough, we were being graciously offered a chance to serve *despite* our failings and flaws.

After a trip to Hong Kong to get new (tourist) visas, we returned to Henan to say farewell to our skateboarding friends, our other friends in the community and, of course, the local staff and children in the Welfare Centre. A friend from among the office staff agreed to help us to find a vehicle and to drive for us – he saw it as an adventure and planned to visit other provinces on the return journey. We paid for a train ticket for his wife so she could join him in Chengdu. It took us a couple of hours to pack the small bread van, and eighteen hours to drive across the country to the city where we now live. My wife was excited to formally enrol to study Chinese in a university here, and I have been helping our "friend from PD" with her business since then.

Praise God that I have received a work permit – they are notoriously difficult to obtain. It would not be fair to say that our life has been smooth ever since then, but our experience with that international charity in Henan has helped us to appreciate what a reasonable, kind and patient employer our friend from PD is, and how faithful God has been to us – especially through all of those who have supported us in prayer and financially over the years. As I type this, in recent days, a group has prepared more than 30,000 RMB to give to a good cause, and wanted advice from my current employer in Chengdu about where it could be used. It was decided that it would be spent on new clothing and shoes for all the children in the Welfare Centre in Henan where we used to work. Praise God!

What can I conclude from this chapter of my life, especially with regard to PD? I feel that the team is best described as truly having welcomed me as a family member into their midst. When we say "We're like family" about friends, we too often mean that we get on well with certain people living near to us, but circumstances often change when one person moves too far away, or there is an argument over something or other. Mel and the team truly exercised godly love and grace to me, and loved me as true family, despite my huge mistakes, faults and flaws, abrasive personality and occasional arguments. I felt that they have always loved me and welcomed me, praising my achievements, giving me opportunities to use my gifts, and rebuking me (with love) when needed. Jesus said that we (his followers) will be known for how we love one another, and I truly feel that this love from Mel and the PD team has been a wonderful witness in a world where you can often be left feeling cynical, undervalued, unwanted and ultimately abandoned. Like the awe-inspiring mountains teeming with life, the love that PD have extended to us is a reminder of how great the God we serve is.

Chapter 17

MELODY
FAILURE IS NOT FALLING DOWN

Melody is a shy, kindly, teacher and team member with a golden heart for those struggling to learn. Her Tibetan students clearly identified that she had an empathy for them which made her very popular. I will never forget how, as an act of unselfish service, she washed the clothes of team members outside the Centre in icy cold water. – Mel

I have been to Dengke with the team three times, which has enabled me to have the opportunity to appreciate gorgeous scenery in Tibetan areas and see another way of life, and also to have the chance to work with people from different cultural backgrounds, and learn from them, which indeed has helped me discover more about myself and improve myself – in the meantime expanding my outlook and enriching my life experience. Personally, it is not only a fun adventure, but rewarding and unforgettable, beneficial for my personal growth.

Before I went to Dengke with the team, I had already seen loads of lovely pictures and some interesting videos about this trip from my elder sister Katherine and my brother-in law Phil, who both had been there with the team a few times. At that time I really wanted to venture out, so I asked my sister if she could recommend me to Mel, our team leader whom I had met once in the UK – at my sister's wedding.

But at that time, I was too shy and too unconfident to speak to him very much.

Then my sister told Mel about me, and she also said to me that Mel might interview me over the phone, because it is a routine that he interviews every interpreter. I was so worried about the interview due to my poor spoken English – at that time I was struggling to speak with native English speakers. Therefore, I prepared for the worst possible outcome which would have been failing the interview and so being unable to make it on this trip. A few days later, my sister informed me that Mel said there was no interview for me because we had already met and I was very welcome to join them. I was ecstatic, and really grateful that the team had given me this opportunity.

Later, on the journey, I had the opportunity to talk to Mel, and I asked him why I was the only one among all the interpreters who had not been formally interviewed by him. He replied: because of our previous meeting, and the recommendation of others, we were happy to help you grow. The moment I heard this I was so touched. I feel like there are people in the world who treat others very well, even when nothing is expected.

Undoubtedly, the trip helped me grow up and shaped my character. I learned a lot from the people around me. Take Mel as an example. When I went to Dengke with the team for the first time, we set out from Chengdu and spent the whole day on the bus. It was a long and exhausting trip, then we arrived in Kangding late in the evening. The next day, I heard team members talking about Mel probably having to fly back to Chengdu early in the morning the following day because he had just been informed by Chinese officials working at the embassy that the photo on his passport had some issues, and they needed him to be there to sort out the problem. Personally, I thought it was very annoying, and I felt sorry for him. He had just got to Kangding after a long journey, and now he had to go back to Chengdu immediately, then come back to Kangding again. I did not see him for most of that day, but another team member said he was going to have dinner with us in the evening, and would head back to Chengdu the next morning. Before seeing him, I thought he would look very upset and would complain about it at dinner but, to my surprise, instead he was talking to us with a huge smile on his face as if nothing unpleasant had ever happened. I plucked up the courage to approach him. That was my first time in Dengke with the team. At that time, I was still very shy and diffident. Even so, I still wanted to have a short talk with him to encourage him. Finally, I walked up to him and we had a brief but very nice conversation. I remember clearly that he talked about his son playing the piano in an amusing way, and he used gestures to demonstrate that, which made me laugh. After dinner it was raining a bit outside and I saw Mel dancing in the rain with an umbrella in his hand, singing with joy. The next day he left very early in the morning.

A few days passed and he had still not come back. I was resting in my room in the daytime when suddenly I heard a guy start singing and playing the guitar very loudly. I thought after a while that he would stop, but actually he kept playing and singing for nearly four hours. Finally, I just went out of my room to find out who this "crazy" guy was. Surprisingly, it was Mel! He had come back. He was singing fondly, meanwhile playing the guitar with several Tibetan kids around him. Obviously, Mel's own "live concert" packed them in, and I got packed in with them too!

The way in which he treats issues or sufferings in life has really had a big influence on me. The best way to live is to be positive. He told me the following story. There were two men behind bars who were locked in the same cell. What one person saw was mud while what the other person saw was the stars. The person who saw the mud was very frustrated and pessimistic; however, the other one, who saw the stars, was very positive, and what he was thinking in his mind was how one day he would get out of there and start a new life.

This story encouraged me when I was experiencing difficult times. In 2017, I applied for a UK student visa. I got everything ready. I packed my suitcase, and all my friends and relatives knew I was going to the UK to study. I was very excited while waiting for my visa, however in the end I received a refusal letter which really hit me hard. I felt so confused, so desperate and heartbroken the moment I found out I had been refused. During those days I just cried all the time, I could not stop it, could not switch off the negative thoughts, and was unable to do anything. It was such a difficult time for me and for my family. One day I was crying again on my own and I felt that I could not continue in that way. I thought of Mel's story, and one of Mel's sayings: "Failure is not falling down, it is failing to get up after we have fallen down" – and the memories of some of my best days in life pushed me to stand up. I decided to find out the reason why I had been refused for the visa, and then to reapply. However, this process was far more complicated and difficult than I had expected, and during the whole process I experienced many difficulties and much sadness. But eventually, with the help of my family and friends, I got through it. All the hard work paid off and the visa was granted, although I was already late for my programme in the UK.

I have also learned to be generous and kind to people without wanting anything from them in return. Mel played us a video in the Centre in Dengke which moved me to tears. It was about a senior lady who had leprosy. In the video she was staying in a muddy cave, her body was deformed by the disease, and for me she looked really scary; I could not imagine I would hug her or shake hands with her, but then I saw our team members appear in that black and dirty cave. They sat next to her very closely, holding her hands, talking to her very warmly, with their communication mainly depending on body language due to the language barrier. Although they spoke so little, I saw the huge smiles on their faces and heard their laughter with pleasure. After the video, I heard more about her story from the team. With the help of team members, her leprosy were bandaged, and the team also built her a new house and went to visit her every year until she passed away peacefully. It is such a moving and warm story.

There were countless other things that really touched my heart. One of them concerns Benjamin, one of our team members. I met him on my third visit to Dengke with the team. I remember it very clearly. When we were on the journey back to Chengdu, we visited a tourist hotspot called Xinlong Lake in Ganzi, which is truly a gorgeous place of natural beauty. When we were exploring there, Benjamin spent some time playing with two little poor Tibetan girls. For some reason these two children began arguing with each other, and the older one made the younger one cry. In order to make her happy again, Benjamin took off his necklace with a cross on it, and gave it to her. The poor little girl stopped crying immediately and a huge smile showed on her face. What Benjamin did made me feel so touched because some team members told me that the necklace was very precious and very special to him, and it was quite expensive, and I had noticed that he wore it all the time, but he just gave it for free. He simply wanted to make that poor girl happy, a child whom he had only met ten minutes before, and would probably never see again. Benjamin's generosity and huge love towards that little girl touched me deeply. I think he lives out God's love.

What has also impressed me is that team's persistence and their everlasting big love for the local people in Dengke. They come here every year to help them unconditionally with healthcare, education and construction, and they have continued to do it for over twenty years. I asked Mel why they had such a big love for people – for people they did not even know. He said to me that the love comes from Jesus who is the source of love.

Lastly, I want to share my experiences of teaching, which I really enjoyed. The first time I went there, I taught English to nine teenagers for several weeks. It was my first experience of teaching. At first I felt very nervous but the moment I entered the classroom and saw them, they put me at ease; they were sitting next to each other very quietly, and the look in their eyes was so innocent. It soon became apparent that they were keen to learn. They behaved so well in the class that I felt trusted and respected. Another thing that made me very pleased was that they studied very hard, although some of them felt a bit physically tired during the class due to loads of physical work they had done before the lesson – they were actually doing their best to learn and they did very well.

The third year I went there I was working with other teachers to teach a large group of children. If the truth be told, the kids looked pitiful – their faces, hands and clothes were very dirty. What was worse was that they were not allowed to go outside the temple, and their parents rarely came to visit them. Every time we went there for class, we helped these kids clean their faces and hands at the sink. It really made my heart suffer when I saw some of the children rub their dirty hands very hard against the concrete sink in order to remove dirt from their hands. We stopped them immediately and taught them to use soap to wash their hands. When I saw a team member help a kid blow his nose, it really moved me.

When I used a dry towel to wipe water from a boy's face, he just looked at me with a warm smile at that moment, and I was very happy.

In the class it was a bit difficult to manage so many young children, but fortunately some teenagers whom we had taught before helped us manage them during the class. The children obviously feared their elder brothers, and when in their presence they behaved very well. I remember one elder monk who helped us manage the class. He was called David, and he had been one of my best students the first year I taught there. I noticed that as he was helping us manage the children during the English class he was absorbing the language himself. In other words, he paid attention to what the teacher was teaching, and also repeated the target language quietly with the children. Even after class, he focused on remembering the new words just taught in the class by repeating them in a low voice for a while. Sometimes he even came to me and asked questions like: "How do I say this in English"; "Am I saying this correctly?" He was truly diligent and very keen to learn. Also, he is a positive and warm person; whenever we talked to him there was always a big smile on his face, and every time we needed help he always tried to help.

When the older teenagers were too busy to come to the class to help manage the kids, the children became a bit naughty but were still manageable. We gave them prizes like sweets and toys when they were well behaved and when they did well, and it worked; we also tried to encourage some shy boys to say out loud their ideas in front of their classmates, which helped to increase their confidence. Additionally, it was a huge pleasure to teach them to draw things – they scrambled to show us their drawings after they had finished. And we teachers were totally impressed by their drawings, which were really brilliant and full of imagination. A piece of good news about these kids that I want to share is that the local government has brought them out of the temple and sent them to school. I am really very happy for them.

I want to say thank you to all the team members. Thank you for helping me grow up, and thank you for being so patient and tolerant; thank you for all your kind help, and thank you for being such great friends, with whom I have had so much fun.

Chapter 18

SEAN
MY JOURNEY TO FAITH

Sean's story is so uplifting. I first met him in Chengdu back in 1990 when we were putting the Hovercraft Team together. He has become a wonderful, enthusiastic, inspirational international Bible teacher, although back then he had no faith at all. What joy to see how the Lord has changed him, and the Holy Spirit now uses him to preach the Good News all over the world. – Mel

It was close to the time of sunset. I went out of the Tibetan style "Friendship Centre" built by the British Christians and walked to the new memorial and museum of General Dengma (a historical Tibetan warrior and leader). I was in this small Tibetan village called Luoxu, or Dengke before it changed its name a few years ago (I am still used to calling it Dengke). After taking a few photos of the memorial, I walked towards the river. It is called the "Jinsha River", the Chinese name for this section of the Yangtze near its source. I stood there with a lot of emotions in my heart – this was the site where we (the expedition team) had camped with our tents twenty-eight years earlier.

This was the summer of 2018. A few days earlier I had flown from my home in a Baltimore (US) suburb to my hometown of Chengdu, Sichuan in China. Then I flew to the Tibetan city of Yushu in the Qinghai Province, and spent a few hours on an *ad hoc* trip by rented minivan to the little town of Dengke. I had come to join the Project Dengke 2018 team and spend a few days with them. It was also a re-visit and a reunion because I had been there with the first British hovercraft expedition in 1990, although only one member of the 1990 team (Mel Richardson, the "nutty professor") was there this year.

While listening to the sound of running water in the river, I thought about how the trip to this exact place nearly three decades earlier had impacted me and changed my life. I thought about how it influenced my spiritual journey from being an atheist to being a Christian. I could not but marvel at God's grace and providence.

Twenty-eight years ago, I was a young professional in the city of Chengdu working for a chemical industry research institute as a polymer scientist. That was one year after the so called "June 4th incident" as it was described by some officials in China. At that time, I might have looked like a "normal" young man on the outside, but I had a lot of pain and struggles deep in my heart. Without doubt that "incident" had a very profound impact on me.

I was born into a Chinese intellectual family. Both my parents graduated from the Huaxi Medical University, which was a Christian medical school established by Western missionaries before the communist era (my parents entered the university after 1949 and were atheists). After their graduation, they were "assigned by the Party" to a very rural, remote and poor Tibetan area in Sichuan (in the same Garze Autonomous Tibetan Area as Dengke is in) and worked there for more than twenty years. They spent the best years of their lives serving people there as medical doctors while living a very hard life.

I was raised by my grandma in the city of Chengdu so I could get an education. I learnt and knew at a very young age that I had to study hard, to get outstanding scores and to enter college if I wanted to escape from having to end up in the poor Tibetan area. This became the whole purpose of my life and I studied very hard. In 1982, I fulfilled my dream and entered Fudan University in Shanghai, which is one of the best universities in China (nicknamed "China's Yale"). I was only sixteen when I left my hometown to pursue higher education in the city of Shanghai, a thousand miles away.

All the education I could get in China was imbued with heavy atheistic teachings. Fudan University was known for its academic openness and "Westernisation". While in Fudan, I started to become very interested in Western thought and culture (probably more than subjects in my chemistry major), and began to build up a self-centered worldview and life philosophy out of the influence of secular Western thought. By then I had already doubted and rebelled against the "official" communist ideology, but I was not seeking faith deeply. I thought my faith was: "I do not believe in anything."

After graduation, I went back to Chengdu and started to work in the research institute. I entered the real world without a fixed faith or a matured worldview. On the one hand, I felt lost and aimless, and learnt to be "just like everyone else", wasting time and damaging my own health with "entertainments" such as playing mahjong (with gambling) all night or drinking *bai jiu* (Chinese hard liquor) to get drunk. On the other hand, deep in my heart, I was unwilling to sink like others because I thought I still had a little remainder of the traditional Chinese intellectual style, i.e., Confucian ideals and ambitions. Those ideals and ambitions were not clear, yet I believed that at least I had the desire to be a good and useful man in the society and to make contributions to my country.

When the June 4th event happened, I was on the street of Chengdu with many young students and intellectuals. I was excited and actively involved in the movement. Tragically, the flame of our patriotic enthusiasm was quickly put out by cruel reality (similar suppression took place in Chengdu as in Beijing). With the feeling of miserable disillusionment, my heart sank to deep darkness and hopelessness. Without a faith, I was not able to face the reality and I could not find an answer to my heart's questions, and life became meaningless and unbearably painful. I was totally lost and broken spiritually.

I tried hard to escape this feeling of being lost by seeking money and pleasure, but I totally failed to get any real satisfaction from either. Moreover, the surroundings around me were showing me how treacherous and dark human hearts could be every day. I started to realise that "the heart of the problem is the problem of the heart", and how insignificant and pitiful I was myself. With all those incurable weaknesses, I was unable to go beyond myself, let alone to practise the Confucian idealism of "cultivation of personality, regulation of family, order of the nation, and peace and harmony of the world".

In the spiritual pain and thirst, I began to realise the desperate need for a transcendent faith. I started to seek philosophical and religious knowledge. I read a lot about things of a "spiritual" nature, which ranged from Western philosophy to traditional Chinese beliefs, and even included things like *Qi Gong* and fortune telling. Occasionally, I would find a little spark of human wisdom in those writings, but they did not give me any significant answers. Some of my readings were related to Christianity, but most of them were very negative, criticising and even attacking Christianity as a superstitious religion or imperialist tool. Only a few books introduced Christian thoughts as one kind of Western philosophical or cultural resource. One of those books was authored by Dr Liu Xiaofeng, who was later deemed to be a leading "cultural Christian". The book was entitled *Salvation and Carefree-ness*, and in it the Christian worldview was compared with other Western and oriental philosophies and cultures. In a strange way, this book created some affinity and a good impression of Christianity in me.

At the same time, God also gave me a few opportunities to know some Christian friends, although there were so few of them in China. Then came my encounter with the British hovercraft expedition. In 1990, with my English speaking ability, I took some tests and got a licence to lead tourist groups as an interpreter guide. One day, on the campus of Huaxi Medical University, I met a few members of the British team, and chatted with them. (One of them was Gwyn Davies-Scourfield, and a picture of me talking with him on that day appears in Dick Bell's *To the Source of Yangtze*.) They were very friendly with me and we saw each other a few more times to practise my English on them. I learned that the team would use hovercraft to go upstream on the Yangtze to the source of the river, and to access the Tibetan areas along the banks of the river there. Beside scientific investigations, they would send medicines and technologies to those remote areas as humanitarian aid by means of this unique way of transportation. Within the group they had a polymer science and engineering team led by Mel Richardson, and a medical team led by "Dr Ray" (Rachel Grace Pinniger).

Later, the head of a mountaineer group in a Chinese geography research institute came to me and asked if I would take a temporary job as the interpreter for him, and join them as they accompanied and assisted the British expedition team in the Garze-Shiqu area. Garze, Tibetan, medical, polymer…, all these words naturally bring upon my heart connections to my background, and I was more than willing to take the job, although I dared not tell my boss at my research institute. (Those were the days when Deng Xiaoping had just opened China's door to the world, and there arose the first wave of

Chinese intellectuals taking a "second career" to make extra money, which had been forbidden before.)

So I went on the journey to Dengke with the British team and their Chinese company. I soon learnt that the British side was a team consisting mostly of Christians, and they had to face a lot of difficulties and challenges in Garze. Not only did they have to face the extremely harsh geographical environment in the areas near the source of the Yangtze, but they also had to deal with the most frustrating bureaucracy and materialist greed of the Chinese side. It even made me lose heart and patience and get angry. However, I saw with my own eyes how these Christians prayed and trusted their God to enable them to face the difficulties, and how they showed their Christian love, not only to the people they helped (mostly the Tibetans), but also to those who made it difficult for them – with forgiveness and understanding. I became the team's friend, and in many things I was obviously on their side instead of the Chinese side.

I saw how they worshiped on Sundays in their tents on the Qinghai-Tibet Plateau (with Mel playing guitar for the hymns). But, more impressively, I saw how Doctor Ray gave vaccinations to little Tibetan kids, and how the team talked to a few Tibetans with leprosy and prayed for them, much to the dismay and fear of the Chinese side. I saw the British gentlemen physically labour hard to remove rocks that blocked the road. I saw how kind the team members were to the Tibetan villagers and how much they desired to help the Tibetans by building a simple bridge or a humble house. The British Christians' positive attitude to life and their unwavering faith in God gave me such a wonderful and powerful testimony during the more than one month's time I lived and worked together with them, even though they did not get much time to tell me about God and study the Bible with me.

The expedition was later broadcast in Britain and on CCTV (Central TV, the national station of China), including scenes of their Sunday worship on the high land by the river. I was punished by the research institute by announcing on the big PA system to hundreds of my colleagues my mistake and the official condemnation, for going beyond my vacation days (which was because of delay that was caused by a big snow storm) and not telling the truth about the trip. But as the Chinese idiom says, I also "got goodness out of misfortune". A beautiful young lady was in the audience and was impressed by my ability to commit such a "crime". I later managed to date her and today she is my wife. More important than that is the British Christians' good witness, which cancelled out a lot of my preconceived misunderstandings and aversion towards Christianity, paving the way for my conversion.

After the expedition, a young friend of mine told me that he had become a Christian, and invited me to one of their house church Bible study gatherings. I was amazed to see a group of young intellectuals with a similar background to mine pray, sing hymns, study the Bible and share together. However, at that time, I knew almost nothing about God and the Bible, and my good impression of Christianity was only on the cultural and intellectual levels. I did not even think about a personal relationship with God and what it would mean for my life.

In August 1992, I moved to the United States to pursue graduate study (in chemistry) at the University of Alabama and to seek my "American Dream". Being able to "make it" abroad was not easy at all for a young Chinese intellectual. Besides the academic challenges (only the very top ones with exceedingly good TOEFL and GRE scores could get the admission and financial aid), it was extremely difficult to get the passport from the Chinese authorities (especially because I was involved in the June 4th event) and the visa from the American Consulate. I spent four days and four nights in front of the U.S. Consulate in Chengdu, and nearly missed my I-20 form for the visa (the replacement did not reach my hands until the last day before my interview with the Consulate). Thinking back today, it is clear that I was able to move to the United States only because God's loving hand was working behind everything.

The period after I arrived in Alabama for the first time was very tough, since I had to endure loneliness away from my family and my newly wedded wife, and to cope with new life in a strange land. During that time, I got much help from some fellow Chinese graduate students and their families, most of whom I soon found out to be Christians, young in their Christian lives. They picked me up from the airport on day one, gave me rides to do shopping, invited me to their homes for Chinese meals, picked up an old mattress others had thrown away for me to use as a bed (there was no furniture in my apartment in the beginning), and offered much other help. They took me to their Bible studies and I got to know many other Christian friends – Chinese and American. Their loving deeds and kind help brought a lot of warmth to me, and I was greatly touched by the love they lived out, which I knew had to come from their Christian faith. The peace and joy from their lives were so real and inspiring, and just as in the case of my experience with the British expedition team, it again caused me to desire to have such a life.

The Bible studies in the Chinese Christian Fellowship in the small southern college town gave me much-needed opportunities to learn about the basic but accurate doctrines of Christianity. In the beginning I had tons of questions to ask, and was quite a difficult and tough seeker. Fortunately the Bible studies were very open, and the Christian friends responded to my harsh, opinionated and provoking questions with much patience and wisdom. My knowledge and understanding increased quickly with all the debates and discussions. I started to realise that I had a lot of misunderstanding and prejudice about Christianity, and I had to overcome many obstacles out of my atheistic and rationalist thinking paradigm. The profound thinking and discussion which took place on issues such as the truth of the Bible, creation versus evolution, faith and reason, and Christianity versus other religions and cultures etc., convinced me that the Christian belief is true, and broke my intellectual stronghold bit by bit. The Bible and Jesus' teachings had an even greater impact on my seeking heart.

But the greatest factor of all was the Christian love that Christians had demonstrated in their actions. It was shocking and very thought-provoking to me. I had grown up in the communist culture of hatred, which taught us to hate our enemy in the class struggle. Mao famously said, "There is absolutely no love in this world without reason." But by the Yangtze River in the Tibetan village, and in the little college town of the U.S. South, I did experience and witness a kind of love that has no worldly reason. I knew that it was impossible that I could repay the love and caring that had been given to me by my Christian friends. I knew that they did what they did purely out of Christian charity, as a true expression of their faith and their values. They were first loved and saved by God. Their real testimony is strong evidence of the biblical truth.

On one Sunday, in October 1992, I was attending worship with friends in a local American church (Tuscaloosa First Baptist Church). I do not remember much about the details of what the pastor preached that day, but my heart was so touched by God that tears filled my eyes. I realised what a sinner I was, and was strongly moved by Christ's love to turn to God. When the pastor asked people who had just decided to accept Christ as their Saviour and Lord to come to the front, I stood up as if I had lost control of myself, and I walked to the front and held the pastor's hands. I told him I wanted to accept Christ as my Saviour and Lord right there and right then. Soon after that, I was baptised in the same church.

A few years ago, I was surfing on the Chinese Q&A website of Zhihu (which is similar to Quora, but arguably better, and influential among Chinese intellectuals). One answer to the question "Under what circumstances did you believe in God?" caught my attention. It was written by a Chinese man in the film-making industry, who called himself Mr Luo Deng (a pen-name). Mr Luo said in his answer that his spiritual journey was influenced by a group of British Christians he had come across in Garze. He said that the British team had been going to Dengke to do charity work, and he was so moved by their love and faith. I immediately realised that he was talking about the same group as the 1990 expedition team, because I knew Mel had led teams to Dengke after the first expedition for many years. I was very excited to see another man with the same experience as mine. I contacted Mr Luo Deng privately and also answered the same question, sharing my own story. Later, another "netter" commented under my answer and said that she had had the same experience too when she worked with the team as an interpreter. During the 2018 Dengke trip I met more interpreters for the team who had become Christians. Apparently, serving as an interpreter on the Project Dengke team has been greatly used by God as a means of evangelising young Chinese men and women!

I was very moved by the stories on Zhihu. Luo Deng's answer got tons of "likes" and people have most appreciated one sentence in it. What he said can be translated literally into

English as: "I believe that the best evangelism is the lifestyle of a Christian." During the 2018 Dengke Project trip, I had the opportunity to share with the team my conversion story and encourage the teammates by using scripture (I used Matthew 5:13–16 which calls Christians to be salt and light in the world) as well as Mr Luo's words – to make the point about the significance that the Project has concerning evangelism.

Back to my own journey of faith. Baptism was only the beginning of my new spiritual journey. My life was greatly changed after I became a Christian, even though I was not always fully aware of it. My worldview and values were transformed by the Word of God. The self-centredness, self-righteousness and denial of God's existence were replaced by the repentance of my sins, obedience to God and a thankful heart. I had sought the meaning of life with such pain, and I was now able to know the true and only God, the Creator of the universe and keeper of our lives, through Jesus Christ. I am able to have a close relationship with God through prayer and studying his Word, and experiencing his guidance in my daily life. I can now experience the peace and joy that transcend surroundings – and the more abundant life that Christ gives us – just as the British team did. My wandering heart has found the ultimate anchor, and my lost soul has found its eternal home.

That does not mean that my journey after conversion was all smooth, or that my spiritual growth did not take time. After I graduated from the University of Alabama with a Master of Science degree in 1995, I started working in the chemical industry in the U.S., and I worked in that field for 16 years, most of the time as an R&D technical manager. Later, my wife and I had two sons (born in 1996 and 2003 respectively). I went through many difficulties and challenges in my marriage, my family, my career and in my service both inside and outside the church.

But the Lord is faithful and his grace is sufficient. Many things have happened in my life. I have learned in my career and in my family life, as well as my serving on the Internet and in the Chinese churches (I have worshipped and served in a number of Chinese churches in the US). I have learned from my mistakes and failures, and God has let me grow in various areas of my life. The journey has been filled with my weakness, but it has also been filled with God's leading and providence.

One example is my writing "career". I started writing about Christianity on the Chinese Internet in 1995 (when the Chinese Internet was just starting with very primitive technologies) because I felt the need for apologetics involvement, and I have since been active in Chinese cyberspace and new media (Zhihu is but one example), holding dialogue with global Chinese intellectuals, and evangelising with my writings and podcast. In 1996, I joined the Chinese Christian Internet Mission as one of its earliest core co-workers. In 1998, I created the evangelist and apologetics website "Jidian's Links" ("Jidian" being the Chinese *pin yin* for "Gideon", which is my pen name), and this provided resources for apologetics and to explain Christian culture to Chinese netizens.

In 2009, I published my first book in Chinese (a collection of apologetics dialogues with non-believers) in the USA. In 2012, I published my second book (a collection of my blog essays on Christian culture and belief) in China. Today I am known as a writer in China, and I have been permitted to give talks about Christianity in the Christian bookstores and coffee houses in many Chinese cities. After many years of writing on the Internet, I am regarded as one of the earliest "Internet missionaries" on the Chinese Internet, both by Chinese intellectuals and by the Chinese communist government – I was named as one of "the most influential (by which they meant 'dangerous') Internet missionaries" in an official paper on a Communist Youth League Central Committee journal warning the Chinese public about the "invasion of Western ideology under the disguise of religion".

I also became a core author for *Overseas Campus (OC)*, a well-known evangelical magazine for Chinese intellectuals, founded in the U.S. in the same year as I became a Christian (1992). In 2011, I was called by God to make a career change to serve him full-time and I joined the Overseas Campus Ministries (OCM) to lead the ministry's Internet mission. (I responded to God's calling in this area for the first time at a Campus Crusade for Christ conference, way back in 1993.) I have since helped establish multiple new media products, such as the electronic magazine *e-OC*, the OC WeChat Public Account (which had 70,000 subscribers before being shut down by the Chinese authorities in December 2018), the OC Fuyin website (ocfuyin.org, *fuyin* being the Chinese phonetic of "the gospel"), and the evangelistic "Jidian's Chat" podcast (http://ocfuyin.org/category/jdlt). I also lead the work of the paper magazine of *OC* as its Chief Editor. It is purely by God's grace that I have become a full-time Christian worker in the media and new media from a scientific background.

Today my work at OCM goes far beyond writing, recording, editing and project management. I have continued to give evangelistic talks in Chinese churches in North America and Asia (China, Hong Kong, Japan, Malaysia, Taiwan, etc.) Because of my background in science, I started speaking on "science versus Christian faith" in China as early as in 2000, and now my evangelistic talks include many other topics. I have been an evangelist speaker and preacher for Chinese churches in North America and Asia. I also give training on apologetics, Christian life, discipleship, evangelism, and how to minister to students and returnees, among other areas. I have served as speaker in various Christian conferences. In my local church (Chinese Bible Church of Howard County, Maryland, USA), I serve by leading Bible studies and teaching Sunday school. I am also studying Theology at the Reformed Theological Seminary Global, working towards an MAR degree while working full-time. In 2018, I joined the new TGC (The Gospel Coalition) Chinese team as a volunteer translation proofreader. In April and October of 2019, I was to go to Glasgow (UK) to serve for three to four weeks each time, helping a Chinese church's student ministry there. I look forward to many more years of serving our Lord with my gifts, all of which are from him in the first place.

Looking back on my spiritual journey, I find myself in awe and thankfulness for God's grace toward me. I believe that it is not by any "coincidence" but by the leading of God's own loving hands that I have become what I am today. My story is just another testimony of God's amazing grace, infinite love and great power. I pray that I will be endowed with the faith and strength to serve God and follow Christ all my life.

Chapter 19

ROYAL
I WAS DEEPLY MOVED

Royal is a very generous young Chinese girl with an extraordinary love story. She was accidentally knocked over by a guy in a Jeep who, horrified, rushed her off to hospital. Later they found out they were both believers, fell in love and got married. Knowing how she loves her smartphone and earpiece, I was tempted once to ask them both: "Who was not paying attention prior to the accident?" You will have to ask them individually to get their replies. I thank her for her kind words, which I really do not deserve. I give all the glory to the Lord. – Mel

My English name is Royal and I was a translator and interpreter for Project Dengke in 2018 and also during earlier years. I have been on Mel's team three times. It was and is a huge pleasure for me to be able to join such a wonderful group.

Several years ago, when I was a middle school student, I first met Mel by chance when I presented him with a gift from the headmaster. Later we exchanged emails about charity work. He always encouraged me and I learnt more about our "crazy" Professor and Team Leader and all about Project Dengke. At that time, I searched about the Project on the Internet and began to realise how much Mel did, and how devoted his team were to Tibetan people. I was deeply moved and made the decision that I had to join the team.

Currently, one cannot find anything on Chinese websites because of Government action – Mel can explain this better than me. Finally, I got the opportunity to join at the age of eighteen and it changed my life because I started to learn about and know God. It was so great to have these friends in the team. They told me about the Lord and how to know him and how to let him lead my life. In Project Dengke we really have had so many wonderful times. Would you like to know what we did in the team? Here are some examples related to another town we visited. We helped the local people to rebuild a kindergarten and we provided many teaching tools for them. We created an English Corner for the primary school children, and British guys like Lauro played football with them and gave them presents and books. The people loved Lauro so much.

After so many years we now have lots of Tibetan friends. So we have many visitors to our Centre and we visit them as well, when we have time. We enjoy singing Christian songs and praying for and with them. Sometimes we can help them with more practical problems. Mel is definitely the most warm-hearted person I have ever met in my life. He really is a great man and a great Team Leader. I am so grateful that he invited me several times to join his Project Dengke Team. I would be willing and delighted to join again. Wouldn't you like to be one of us so that you too can help the people in western China? They really need more friends like Mel and the other members of the Team.

Chapter 20

WILLOW
A TURNING POINT IN MY LIFE

Willow is a delightful, thoughtful person. With her impeccable English she has always been a great asset to the team, even more so now she has come to faith. She has come through some tough, unfair confrontations with officials but stood fast with dignity and quiet determination. – Mel

Greetings from Chengdu. I initially joined Project Dengke five years ago and I have been to the mountains three times. In 2018, I was privileged to go back to the mountains again and it was as big a thrill as always.

The first time I joined the Project, I was trying to find out who God was because I was still confused. But after witnessing the characteristic good behaviour as well as many of the good deeds that the Project members have been doing for more than twenty years in that small village, I was sure that the God they believe in is the one I should believe in too. I became a Christian soon after.

Joining the Project was a turning point in my life and this year is also very important because, after being a Christian for four years, I think at this point in my life God wants to show me more about what a true Christian is like. I went back to the mountains. I worked and served together with various members including Mel, Carey and John. I saw that they were doing everything they could to help the people, and they were trying in every way to praise God. Sometimes they made me feel ashamed about myself, but this experience is very important. It reminds me to improve my ability to serve. I just want to say thank you to all the Project members for their encouragement and their support. I genuinely hope that more people can know about Project Dengke and I will continue praying for the Project. Thank you for taking the trouble to read this.

Chapter 21

DAVID VERNON
MISSING THE TOILETS

It is a joy to have David on the team. Apart from being a doctor, he has a unique style of dry Scottish wit. Of course, he fits my crew criterion of 5Cs – Christ Centred, Committed and Completely Crackers – but his sense of humour is an added advantage. In reality, the loos in the mountains can be dire. Without seeing the funny side of situations one can become "dead in the water", excuse the pun. – Mel

Our readers will be aware that in the early days there was a good deal of discussion and concern about the adequacy of the toilet facilities en route to Dengke, and also of the provision once there.

Indeed, this was an observation made in the content of the first book, *Nearest the Sun*. In fact, in Appendix A of that book is the Dengke Loo Song – sung, I believe, to the tune of the Kangding Love Song or a 12-Bar Blues.

My first trip was in 2006 at Easter. The team was very largely medical and the plan was to consider the possibility of providing more medical facilities in the second wing of the as then unfinished Friendship Centre. With Dr Wujin, we were wondering whether on the ground floor there could be a minor surgical theatre, which might deal with obstetric procedures, as well as minor emergency surgery. We had hoped to provide improved consulting facilities and also, perhaps, a simple laboratory. In the end, this scheme did not come to fruition.

As I have said, there was something of an obsession with bodily needs and the relevant facilities. There was then a rather basic male and female toilet building, which accommodated four or five persons at a time who would have to be in rather close proximity, squatting over a hole in the floor, separated by low partitions. "Basic and uncleaned" would be a flattering description. But it is surprising how well one adapts!

As we were leaving, one young doctor, who became a Paediatric Anaesthetist, commented to a more senior colleague, soon to become a Consultant Microbiologist, "I am going to miss these toilets." This brought the reply, "Many people have!" How smart and how true!

Chapter 22

JANET KOLL
SHOOT ME FIRST

Some years ago, I heard some of my team were rather concerned that I had invited Godfrey and Janet Koll, a couple in their 80s, to join us. Reading between the lines, I am guessing they were saying: "Mel has really blown it this time!" As it turned out, they coped with both the journey and the altitude extremely well, although not without some discomfort, of course. Their stories and witness to the team were immensely powerful, as the following story will illustrate. Godfrey is now in glory but his legacy remains.

– Mel

My name is Janet and I am married to Godfrey and I would like to tell you how the Lord and the angels preserved his family back in 1940. Godfrey was eight and his sister was ten, and he was living with his parents in China.

The Japanese invaded the city, and the whole Chinese church took refuge in their home. The story is that the family, including Godfrey and his sister, stood outside the front door, confronting the Japanese soldiers as they advanced. Godfrey is reputed to have said, "My sister and I will stand in front, so that if the Japanese shoot us then we will not have to watch them shoot you." They stood there, and as they prayed we believe the Lord and his angels prevented the Japanese from shooting any of them, or any in the Chinese church. As a result, he and I met, and we were married for fifty years. I thank the Lord for having preserved his life – and the lives of his family too, all those years ago.

Chapter 23

PHIL MARTIN
I WAS WELL AND TRULY HOOKED

My buddy Phil and I meet, with others, early each Monday morning for our "Men in the Shed" prayer time. We have all said we would not miss it for the world; what a great way to start the week. If you have never had the joy of meeting together with fellow believers, and tangibly felt the quiet certainty of God's presence, you do not know what you are missing! Get stuck in! – Mel

In 2005, I stared at the book given to me by my Mum, and as I looked blankly at its cover I read the phrase "An enthralling story of courage, adventure and commitment" – Sir Cliff Richard OBE. I was studying the montage of photos and wondered why Mum had felt that this should be a book that I needed to read. Had I not had enough adventures in my life? To name just two: a previous short-lived failed marriage, a spell under the judgemental eyes of a Crown Court because of some adolescent high jinks that caused serious injury to a friend.

I picked up the book and read the title and author out loud: *Nearest the Sun* by Mel Richardson. I flicked through the chapters to try and get a sense of whether this was something I needed to be bothered with. A book handed to me by my ever-loving, devoted, Christian mother. What would be contained within those pages that she thought, after years of prayers held at her church (I say church, more of a small gathering of people in a house who meet regularly on a Sunday) that God had not managed to fix so far?

The audacity of Mel and a group of Christians to go to communist China in 1990 was breathtaking. They took on the mighty Yangtze River in a tiny hovercraft, overcoming all kinds of difficulties including, in a snow storm, climbing on top of the crippled craft as it went along, using a gloved hand as a windscreen wiper. BBC South Today showed clips of dangerous jagged ice on both sides of them as they broke the Guinness World Altitude Record for Hovercraft. They were the first people in history to navigate to the source of the Yangtze River against the flow. The Tibetans held out hands of friendship to help his team, and Mel promised an urchin girl, Udren, and an old goatherd, that he would come back to help them. He has done that every year since. On another occasion, the driver of a lorry went off the side of an extremely hazardous cliff. Mel prayerfully decided how to work out a plan for how they could get down safely. Technicians and medical people led further prayer. Thousands of feet below they found this guy trapped by his legs in his lorry and they had to use a wheel jack to get his leg free and eventually get him to hospital. I began to think: What am I doing with my life? How many people would willingly put themselves in such precarious situations?

After reading the book I put it down and by now I was well and truly hooked. I convinced myself that this would be my next escapade. Little did I realise that, in comparison to all my other "escapades", the impact of this book was going to change my life in a way that I was least expecting. But what possible justification or reason did I have to travel to this far-off place in a remote part of China/Tibet, poverty-stricken and under-developed? After all, despite everything, I had a successful renovation business, I was no longer a wage slave, and I was surrounded by all the modest comforts that life had to offer.

Mel was a member of the church that my Mum attended, and after one of his trips he talked about an exciting incident, and to those people that know Mel, this was only one of many. This incident, he recalled, involved an electric gate which barred the entrance to the Fellowship Centre that he, and other volunteers, went to build, fix, and refurbish on an annual basis. It was built with a vision to support the local community. One morning, Mel approached the Centre, along with his wife Ci Ci, and reached out to the gate to enter the complex. He was immediately injected with a 240 volt electric shock. It seemed like there was a call for an electrician. Mel told my Mum that he was looking for a volunteer to come out to Dengke on their next trip to help fix these gates and also to do some much-needed electrical work at the nearby hospital. And there it was – that was my calling!

Many months later, I found myself examining the electrics at the Centre and the nearby hospital. Already suffering from altitude sickness, I barely had the energy, physically or mentally, to handle what was before me. I joked to John (one of the other volunteers), "If I had enough puff I would leg it!" This was going to be a big job.

The hospital was in a terrible state: roof leaks, rotten floors and general filth. We entered one of the buildings and there was rubbish and also ashes all over the concrete floors. A couple of wood-burning stoves had been discarded in the corridor. We passed them and headed for the end room. Sat on a mattress on the floor was this leprous sixty-year-old lady. She could not walk but crawled around on her knees, her bones exposed through her skin. She was partially blind and only had stumps for her hands. My heart was pulled from out of my chest. She was the most pitiful sight I had ever seen.

Our interpreter Katie, and Val our physiotherapist, sat with her and asked her how she was. She replied, "I do the best that I can." I was told that the only physical contact she has is when our volunteers arrive at the Centre every year. Val and Katie gave her a big hug and, for a short while, I held her disfigured hand. We then moved on to another part of the hospital to continue our "rounds". At this point, I started to miss my family.

I reflected on my visit when I returned home. I had an overwhelming sense of admiration for the contentment that the people in this small area of Tibet had. Their hospitality was humbling, and, from a materialistic point of view they had very little but gladly gave. Why was it that they seemed to be so much more content than I was? I was living in one of the richest countries in the world with no material needs or physical challenges, but I was as miserable as sin itself. Deep in my heart, I knew that what I needed was Jesus in my life. And so it was that He found me.

A New Life

Becoming a Christian is one thing, but explaining it to others is another! After all, our families and friends know everything about us, "warts and all". Again, my Mum prayed for me but this time I was praying for myself – and those around me.

Enter the second book that helped me: *Husbands and Fathers: Rediscover the Creator's Purpose for Men* by Edwin Louis Cole. After reading this book I looked back on how I behaved as a husband and a Dad. I was absent most of the time, busy working on one renovation project after another. There was no stability in our lives as we were moving from one place, renovating it, then moving to the next. My wife had no support from me. No wonder it was difficult. My family was heading towards the iceberg of doom without anyone at the helm to steer the ship off that trajectory.

My first resolve, with God's help, was to stop arguing; to be more present and involved; to sit and listen to what was going on in my family and not to answer back. Home life is a lot calmer now. I take my concerns to the Lord and ask for his help, guidance and wisdom. I know from my own experience that my prayers are heard and answered. One day the results will be revealed. One day!

I look back to the day when I volunteered to go to Dengke and saw how delighted my Mum was that I had decided to go. This was her answer to all those prayers. It is an expensive trip and I received financial support from that very small church. One generous lady, Mary, wrote me a little note: "May God bless and use you as you work in Dengke." Amen to that!

Chapter 24

VAL THOMSON
TWO DEAR LADIES

Val Thomson is one of the longest-serving members of my team. I gave her the name "Miss Dengke" because she seems to know just about everybody in the town. Because of her heart of gold, everyone loves her. Originally a physiotherapist, she has time for each and every person.

– Mel

Shintso

"Drashedele! Drashedele! Drashedele!" shouted and laughed Shintso, clapping her almost fingerless hands, whilst wildly shaking her arms in welcome and bouncing up and down on her knees. We had become like family to her now.

For me, it began in 1992 when I was given permission by the local hospital to visit this wonderfully spirited lady, so disfigured by the dreaded disease of leprosy, even though the disease had long-since been cured by medication. "She lives over there," the village ladies pointed, "on the hill over the valley" calling, "Shintso! Shintso!" Within a few moments a figure could be seen on the horizon, waving vigorously. After a steep climb, we arrived at her clay-built cave-like dwelling. Inside, on the floor, was her mud-based bed with some bedding, a clay range and blackened kettle, tin cup and flask; there was no room for much else, nor even space to stand up. Yet outside was the most beautiful small, walled garden, with brightly coloured orange and yellow flowers.

Shintso so loved flowers.

We visited regularly, wanting to bring the love of Christ to her, touched by her awful suffering yet cheerful demeanour. We encouraged her in the care of her disfigured limbs, to try to prevent further disability, reinforcing what she had been taught by the local hospital. On one visit our team dentist removed a decayed tooth which was giving much trouble, to Shintso's great relief! Invariably, a little crowd of interested women and children would appear and Shintso could be heard feistily asking them to leave. At other times she would revel in the attention and talk excitedly to them. On some visits, for privacy, we crawled to join her in her home – a move that shocked the locals for we were told that no Tibetan would dare go into the home of someone who had suffered from leprosy. She was such a wonderful character. We always enjoyed our visits to her, with some banter, humour, and sharing of pictures, and stories of our families, countries and culture. Over the years, we introduced many people to her, especially those who would be able to visit when we were not able to do so, and so we became like an extended family.

But what of her story? We were told that her own family was originally from "over the river", i.e. Tibet, but that she had been brought up by other relatives in the hamlet near where she now lived, until she contracted leprosy in her early teens and then she became an outcast. She did not seem to harbour any bitterness, but seemed to have an acceptance that this was her "fate" in life – that she must have done something awful in a past life and was now reaping the consequences. Such is the lack of hope found in Tibetan Buddhism, and the awful fear created by lack of understanding of the disease of leprosy, and its infliction of disfiguring disabilities. In fact, once the disease is treated, it is no longer transmissible, though the disability may increase injury to limbs affected by the nerve damage and lead to subsequent lack of feeling.

Shintso became well known to our teams and to many other friends over the years. We always visited her frequently when in Dengke. Her life touched countless people as we carried news of her back home after our trips, and many were challenged by the love of Christ shown to her, an outcast.

However it was during the short time that Dr Ray and Marianne were living in the Friendship Centre that she needed most help, to save her sight, and after a real struggle she was eventually admitted to the hospital. A friend of the team painted white her blackened and dirty hospital room. By this time she was also unable to walk, and a low trolley was made for her to sit on, and a wheelchair provided. But even more wonderfully, in the year before, a purpose-built new little home had been built, next to the cave, one in which people could stand up and which had easy access for her. She was thrilled! Whilst staying at the hospital, she was wonderfully cared for by the team, who cooked for her and slept nearby her in her room. (Food is provided by a patient's family when in hospital, and Shintso was afraid of a squatter living in the hospital block where she was.) She was brought regularly to the Friendship Centre for a good wash, time with her friends, singing, music and films. One fond memory I have of her is sitting with others enjoying a meal in the kitchen. One cannot imagine what this must have meant to her, the "outcast" sharing food with those who loved her, off the same plates as all were using.

With love and care she was able to return to her home again. But as time went on she became increasingly frail, and as a deep-seated infection set in, the end was near. She loved photographs of her friends and these would never be far from her; she was always fishing them out when people visited. "I am waiting for my family. They promised they would come. They will come," she told the local friend who was caring for her. And in his goodness, in perfect timing, just before she slipped into unconsciousness, precious friends who were able to communicate with her in her language, arrived. As they sang, ministered and prayed with her, her little home was filled with an overwhelming, wonderful sense of peace and the presence of the Holy Spirit, and so she slipped into eternity where we believe she is now loved and able to praise with outstretched arms.

As a postscript, our team arrived about a week after she had died. At a stop, hours before Dengke, some people in a hamlet asked us if we had heard that a lady with leprosy had died, and that some foreigners had been with her, in her home, and not only that, they had had a small child with them too – in the home of someone with leprosy. Had we heard? Did we know them?

"Yes," said someone who was with us. "I was there, and the child was my child."

Such was the impact of their actions that people in the valley for miles and miles around knew the news. Later, near the site of Shintso's home we met a dear local lady who broke down inconsolably as she saw us. She had latterly been caring for Shintso, till the end.

Tongjia

I cannot but mention another very dear lady, Tongjia, in a very similar situation in the opposite direction from Shintso – an outcast living in a hole in the ground, even smaller than Shintso's cave. She was a quieter, gentler character than Shintso, who as the years went on increasingly seemed to have people around. Perhaps our visits had dispelled some of the fear of her disability. But Tongjia's isolated life also had a huge impact on others, unknown to her, leading at least one person to find Christ. One of our translators testified at her baptism that it was the life of this lovely lady, so marred by the disability of leprosy, that the Lord used to convict her of her hardness of heart and lack of love as she found that, in her pride, she could not approach Tongjia. It exposed the sin in her life that she later repented of, and she wonderfully found Christ as her Saviour. The Lord did not waste Tongjia's terrible suffering, and we pray that he may have also had mercy on her and received her as one of his dearly beloved children into his kingdom.

We believe that our visits bringing the love and care of Christ, few as they were, will not have been in vain. The Lord led us to meet her and Shintso, and we believe this was for an eternal purpose. I cannot forget Tongjia's heart-rending sobs as we hugged her, and wept with her. No words were possible. To have human touch and love was all we could give. Also, the glow of joy as she tasted her first ever banana! As we passed on some new warm clothes and non-perishable food, Tongjia said, "Take them inside or they will be stolen. They are safe inside. No one dares enter my home." So in I crawled. There was only room for one inside. How did she survive on the food brought to her, scraps that would otherwise have been given to the pigs? How did she manage with no hands? How could she possibly haul water up the hill? Her life was unbearably hard, but her beautiful wrinkled smile that lit up her face can never be forgotten.

The Lord touched our lives and changed us through these dear ladies. It was humbling to have our privileged lives so crossed with theirs. There were also others whom we have met over the years, who I will never forget, who were suffering the terrible effects and ignorance surrounding leprosy.

A man with leprosy came to him and begged him on his knees, "If you are willing, you can make me clean." ...

Moved with compassion Jesus reached out his hand and touched the man. "I am willing," he said. "Be clean!" Immediately the leprosy left him and he was cleansed. (See *Mark 1:40–42.*)

… The Lord does not look at the things people look at. People look at the outward appearance, but the Lord looks at the heart. (Taken from 1 Samuel 16:7.)

Who is like the Lord our God, the one who sits enthroned on high, who stoops down to look on the heavens and earth? He raises the poor from the dust and lifts the needy from the ash heap. He seats them with the princes, with the princes of their people… praise the Lord! (Psalm 113:5–8.)

Chapter 25

HUIXI "CICI" RICHARDSON
MY LIFE HAS BEEN CHANGED

This is the story of my dear wife "Ci Ci" who is so precious to me. My equally precious first wife "Jackie" wrote me a letter instructing that it was to be given to me in the event that she died of the brain tumour she was suffering from. After her death, I read with great emotion the kind words she said about me and the two requests. "One, please keep leading Project Dengke; and two, please remarry as soon as possible – you need a wife!" Remarrying was the last thing on my mind but the Lord had other plans. – Mel Richardson

Hi, I am Ci Ci, Mel's Chinese wife. I am so glad that I first met him many years ago. I initially went to Dengke in 2003 as a last-minute emergency interpreter which required me to take time off from my job as a restaurant captain in the five-star Jin Jiang Hotel in Chengdu. This was my first experience of going into such a remote mountainous region of a Tibetan Prefecture. Also, it was my first chance to meet the mainly British Team and see their dedication and love for the local people. In those days, the journey was even more dangerous and difficult than it is now. After this initial experience, I continued helping the team, travelling more than seven times into the area. In particular, I was able to spend long hours negotiating with the then very difficult town mayor (who was subsequently replaced). After a lot of persuasion, I managed to get him to sign off on the documents required to keep the project going.

Journeys are always fun! To the great amusement of the team, I always march unannounced into the kitchen of any wayside cafe to check it is clean and serving fresh food.

Both previously, and currently, one of my most significant tasks has been to find vehicles and drivers, and make appropriate hostel or hotel bookings. It takes a long time to make sure the team are not being "ripped off".

The most important spiritual event in my life has been becoming a born-again Christian. On the long journeys I spent many hours finding out what motivated the team and what they believed. Later one year, Mel invited me to the UK and I travelled around the country staying with various team members whilst he was away for part of the time, speaking at a conference and lecturing at universities in the USA. Their stories really challenged me. Then, finally, it all seemed to come together after I saw the "Jesus film" in my own language. The simple but profound message was *"for God so loved the world that he gave his one and only Son, that whoever believes in him shall not perish but have eternal life."* I immediately admitted my sin, believed Jesus could forgive me, and committed my life to him. Later, Mel asked me to marry him and we now have a lovely 10-year old-son. In the illustrations you will see Mel popping the question (appropriately enough in Dengke), and Kieran playing the drums.

Because my UK church is on the South Coast of England I was baptised in the sea on June 28th 2009 – a very public witness to my faith in Jesus. My daily reading that day from "Streams in the Desert" was part of Rev 4:1 "…..there before me was a door standing open in heaven…." This was a great encouragement to me and a confirmation I had done the right thing.

How happy I am that I took up that offer to be an interpreter all those years ago!

APPENDIX A

EVER STOPPED TO WONDER   PETER CUNNINGHAM
(12 Bar Blues song written by Mel Richardson
adapting words from the original poem)

Ever stopped to wonder, what this life is all about,
Why and where you're going, when your lease on life runs out?
Maybe far too busy, trying hard to reach your goal,
Let me ask you kindly,
HAVE YOU THOUGHT ABOUT YOUR SOUL?

You reach the highest portals, your dreams may all come true,
Wealth and fame and fortune, success may shine on you,
Friends may sing your praises, not a care on you may roll,
What about tomorrow,
HAVE YOU THOUGHT ABOUT YOUR SOUL?

All our days are numbered, although you're riding high,
All us poor old mortals, will one day up and die,
Success and fame and glory, won't be worth the bell they toll
Asking just one question,
HAVE YOU THOUGHT ABOUT YOUR SOUL?

If you've never thought it over, spend a little time today
Nothing more important, will ever come your way,
The joy of sins forgiven, a life that's been made whole,
In the name of Christ the Saviour,
WILL YOU THINK ABOUT YOUR SOUL?

Download MP3 Recording:
https://spaces.hightail.com/receive/gFFFDO6eem
or view on youtube:
https://youtu.be/oSYV_Ah8hNQ
https://www.youtube.com/watch?v=oSYV_Ah8hNQ&feature=youtu.be

APPENDIX B

CYCLING AROUND THE WORLD
MICHAEL ZHANG AND KAREN BENNETT

Project Dengke abounds with ordinary people with extraordinary vision and determination. Not least in this department is Michael Zhang. Would you believe someone who told you: "I have no bike, no experience, no training, no visas, but I am going to cycle round the world for you…"?

No, me neither! I get many people with sincere but impossible ideas about how to help us. Most of their well-meaning aspirations evaporate when reality kicks in. But not this time. I was leading a meeting in Gosport in front of several hundred people when a voice shouted from the back "I want to say something", and Michael marched down to the front. This is a classic leader's nightmare – someone who may want to disrupt a presentation.

I made the instant decision not to try to prevent him. As it turned out he said very graciously: "I want to say thank you on behalf of my country China for wanting to show love and care to people in Dengke." This was such an encouragement to us all. What follows is a description of how he actually did go around the world on a borrowed bike. Prior to his setting off, I asked: "How many weeks have you trained for?"

He replied, "None…I will just do it…." Mel

Summary of his Journey
On 24th April 2004 Michael set off from Midhurst, England and cycled across England, France, Belgium, Holland, Germany, Denmark, Sweden, Finland, Russia, Kazakhstan and China (11 countries). On 2nd November he arrived in Hefei. This journey took him 193 days and covered over 9,000 miles. His bicycle weighed 30kg and his luggage was a further 10kg.

Return Trip Summary

Michael set off from Hefei, China on 19th May, and crossed Canada from Vancouver to Toronto by the end of June. He flew to Manchester and cycled to Midhurst, arriving on 4th August 2005.

The return journey took him just over two months and covered a further 3,000 miles.

All in all, his around the world bicycle trip took him through 13 countries, took nine months to complete, and he covered in the region of 13,000 miles.

His Journey

On Saturday 24th April, Michael set off with his friends Steve Coackley, Adam Dalziel, Steve Gentle and Mick Bennette on a once in a life-time adventure that saw them cycle over 9,000 miles from London to Beijing. For seven months they rode through Europe, Scandinavia, Russia and Kazakhstan before reaching their final destination in China.

They were self-sufficient, with their bicycles being fully laden with all the equipment they needed for the expedition: tents, sleeping bags, clothes, tools, bike spares and basic medical kit. They set out planning to cycle anything from 60 to 100 miles per day with the odd rest day thrown in for good measure.

Michael, whose real Chinese name is Zhang Qiong, came to study in Midhurst, West Sussex, England in December 2001. He planned to ride back to his home country, not only for the adventure and character-building experience, but also to raise money for a Chinese based charity: Project Dengke.

He says: "This is a wonderful place with many nice people and beautiful countryside. I enjoyed the two years I spent here, although I was homesick sometimes. I had a dream to go back to China by land. This dream became a plan of cycling home across Europe, Russia and Central

Asia to east China, from 23rd April to November in 2004. This was a brave and crazy idea. How daunting and tiring it was to investigate the route, get several visas, carefully select equipment, etc. But it was worthwhile for me to do! The lessons and hardship I experienced on this expedition would equip me for my future. When I look back on such an adventure in the years ahead, I will marvel at my own confidence and audacity.

Also, it was a good opportunity to raise funds for a most worthy cause: Project Dengke. I first learned about Project Dengke from Mel Richardson, Glyn Davis and the Team at a "Care and Share Foundation" Conference in Gosport, in 2002. I was amazed that these well brought-up Westerners were willing to do dirty, sometimes dangerous work, in Sichuan Province of Southwest China. Their actions speak loudly about their love for the poor and needy. They planned to construct a building for a long-term base, providing a centre for medical treatment, an orphanage, caring for old people, etc. I am deeply touched by their sacrifice.

The Route

From England...
Michael and his friends cycled along the coastline to Dover, which took two days. They caught the ferry to Calais and cycled through **France** for one day, along the French coast to Dunkirk, Belgium.

Belgium was more pleasant to cycle through, with cycle lanes lined with trees and canals. Less than one day's cycling and they were in **Holland** with its excellent cycle lanes, straight canals everywhere, bridges over canals, old windmills in the countryside and new windmills along the coast.

From Holland, it was on to **Germany** and then a ferry from Travemunde, North Germany, through **Danish waters** to Trelleborg, south **Sweden**.

According to Michael, the weather in Sweden was more changeable than the weather in England. The country seemed totally covered by forest. Trees were everywhere and there were also many lakes in south Sweden.

May 17th saw Michael in Stockholm, capital of Sweden. It had been 25 days since they left Midhurst and he had cycled 1,970 km, averaging about 100 km every day.

From Sweden they caught a ferry across the Baltic Sea to Turku in **Finland**, before heading on to Helsinki and the Russian border.

"I enjoyed the week in Finland. The weather was quite nice. Because my visa for Russia did not start until 1st June, we had nine days to cycle 400km in Finland – 45km a day! There are 140,000 lakes in Finland. We bought fishing stuff. We did not get up until 8 a.m., then writing the diary, reading, etc. We did not set off until 1 p.m.

"After one hour of cycling, we stopped at the lakes to fish for a couple of hours. Then we would carry on the trip, and stop to fish again. In the evening, we camped at the lake side and fished again. So far, we had just caught a tiny fish. By the way, it did not get dark until 11 p.m. and it became bright at 3 a.m.! I thought I should go further north to cross the Arctic Circle to see the sunlight at midnight!"

From Finland on to **Russia**, his ninth country on his trip so far. They headed on to St. Petersburg, about 170 km from the Finnish border, to find no hot water in some hostels but were still able to feel very refreshed after the chilly showers.

"It was about 650 km to Moscow from St Petersburg, which took us a week to cycle. One fifth of this road is very bad and our bikes were shaking when we cycled on some bumpy stretches. Needless to say, it was crazy to cycle into the city centre! The traffic was bad. Also we got five punctures on that day alone, getting into Moscow. I just wanted to leave that big city and go back to the countryside, heading eastward again."

July 1st saw Michael in Kazakhstan.

"I had a bottle of beer to celebrate entering the tenth country of my pedal-2-china charity bike ride. It was Kazakhstan! Now I was in Kostanay for a one-day break. So far I had cycled over 6,000 km, including through the Ural Mountains. That meant that I had finished half of the trip and was nearing China."

After Almaty, the capital of **Kazakhstan**, they turned east toward China. On to Xinjiang, west **China**, and the old silk road.

"Although we were away from the desert, we were still in the wild west. Sandy storms could still come to us. We planned to carry on the old silk road until Lanzhou, then turn northeast across Inner Mongolia to Beijing. We had done 12,000 km since leaving Britain, and it was our fifth month on this trip. We were still 2,500 km from Beijing, and about 4,500 km from Shanghai via Beijing. The rest of this trip could take us another one and a half months. Hey, welcome back to civilisation!"

They went to the Great Wall of China and the Terracotta horses and warriors in Xi'an.

Having cycled through China for almost two months and mostly seeing desert, Michael was pleased to reach Inner Mongolia with the prospect of seeing some grassland very soon. They did not see any grassland until about 1,000 km away from Beijing.

In Beijing, Michael bid farewell to two of his cycling friends who were flying back to Scotland.

"I did not feel sad until this morning that two of our cycling mates (Steve and Micky) are flying back to Scotland. The freedom like that of birds has come to the end for them. The six months together makes us like a family and this long holiday had turned to one kind of life for our guys. Adieu to Steve and Micky."

Flash and Michael would finish the last leg of their charity bike trip from Beijing to Shanghai at the beginning of November.

"I arrived at my home town on 2nd November. Finally, I lost my freedom on a bike like a bird, but I was freed from this Eurasian trip and could do some other things.

"Crossing two continents, spending 193 days (24/4-2/11) on this trip, I am still alive on the surface of this earth. What a miracle! Further, my legs and arms and my face got very deeply suntanned, and I have an athletic shape. When I cycled on the road, I felt: This is a strange place for me and I do not belong in this place. But I lived in China for more than twenty years before I went to England. Will it be difficult for me to settle down here after two years living in Britain?"

The Return Trip

Yes it was, and Michael soon found himself planning his route back to Midhurst, West Sussex, this time via Canada.

In June he and some friends left Vancouver on their bikes, planning to cycle to Boston by crossing North America. He cycled 1,500km, and crossed two provinces, British Columbia and Alberta, cycling through the Rocky Mountains. He still had about 5,000km to cycle to reach Boston.

"Over a 2,000km stretch in the prairies, we came to Thunder Bay, a coastal city by Lake Superior. Almost every Canadian knows the statue of Terry Fox in Thunder Bay. He had one leg but ran for the Hope of Marathon. He said, Dreams are made if only people try.

"It was over 700 km cycling around Lake Superior for us. Lake Superior is the biggest, deepest and coldest lake in the world. There were so many ups and downs on this stretch. Some were very steep. The bad news was that there were no pavement shoulders. It was mad for us to cycle on the same lane with trucks.

"But the scenery around Lake Superior is wonderful. Camping on the beaches, swimming in the shadow, watching the sun rising and setting above that big lake was amazing beyond description."

In the last 800 km stretch, from Sault Ste Marie to Toronto, Michael rode solo, achieving 250km on one day, and he reached Toronto within three and a half days. He "heard one sound in his mind" – stop – so he decided not to go on to Boston, but stopped to do some sightseeing in Toronto with friends.

Michael's idea of sightseeing was to involve a further 700 miles of cycling by going to Niagara Falls and cycling back to Toronto. He also took a trip to Ottawa before returning to Toronto, then flying back to England.

"I landed in Manchester from Canada. And from there, I started my last leg of around-the-world bike trip back to Midhurst, from where I had set off for China the previous April. It was jolly good to have the nice English weather. Not hot and humid. I could cycle through the whole day, even at midday

"So my English-made Dawes bike carried me through thirteen countries, covering about 13,000 miles. I am back to reality!"

Michael now plans to stay in England a bit longer and hopes to do some studying while over here.

His current means of transport – his bicycle, of course!

APPENDIX C

POEMS CELEBRATING GOD'S GRACE
ZANIESHA BULZE

Zaniessha is a sweet young girl from Alverstoke Evangelical Church (AEC) where I worship when I am in the UK. Hearing the stories about God's grace concerning Project Dengke she has written these beautiful poems. Mel

My God, My King

The burdens I've carried you took them away. The life that was
broken you've mended day by day. The hardships I've lived
through showed your grace on my side.
Oh how it amazes me my God is alive.

Your strength you have given me.
In your wisdom I'll hide.
For you've suffered the cost for my foolishness and pride.
Your love is unconditional,
your peace who can comprehend.
Oh how magnificent are your mercies,
my God is with me to the end.

The paths I've chosen weren't the ones you had for me but you
were always there, that still small voice whispering to me. You
gave me your words to guide me along, showing me how to live
right and turning me from the wrong.

So I'll sing songs of praises with the words you impart and my
life will be of worship to you Lord, king of my heart.

The King Who Mends

Jesus saw the beauty in our brokenness.
He broke the chains of sin.
Conquered death to free us so we'll be whole in him.

He mends the scattered pieces, to rend the veil that separated us.
So we can wear his cloak of righteousness
and he could bear the cost.

Jesus saw the beauty in our brokenness.
He came and made a way, bringing light into darkness
so life will be ours today.

He knitted us together, as they nailed him to the cross.
Bringing many souls to trust in him,
God's family his finished work.

In the Image of God

We were created in his likeness to represent his authority,
reflecting his glory and his love for all to see.

We were shaped in his image, formed from the dust, with his
breath in our nostrils his life now apart of us.

We were declared good on the day of creation, perfect in his
eyes, but we rebelled against him and separation was sins
destructive prize.

We were made to love and honour him.
To be apart of his family, us as little children, him a loving
Father providing all that we need.

Jesus My Rescue

My sins are before me
Like the sands on the shore,
Ever present and can't be ignored

Flawed and empty,
Fear and shame are
the words I've carried
and called my name.

Broken and lonely,
Foolishness and pride are
the lies that I've feed on
and now I can't hide.

When I thought it was hopeless
and no one can help.
You came and saved me by giving yourself.

Freedom Through Grace

Through your death and resurrection you've bought freedom
from sin, for a world walking in darkness, so that life may reign.

The ones who trust you and call on your name have life everlasting through your grace, exchanged for their shame.

Where sin once was winning, now grace has taken hold, of the
mantle as the prophets had foretold.

Through you Lord Jesus, grace has abound now sin has no hold
and death has no crown.

Fig. 1
Mel with Rinpoche, leader of the monks

Fig. 2
Carey, Pacific, Janet and Melody teaching Monks
Chinese and English

Fig. 3
*Abigail, Janet, Pacific, Ben, Melody, Rachel and Mel –
running conversation and guitar classes*

Fig. 4
*Udren, Demo, Mel, "Old Goatherd", Ringa, and Rob
plus the original Project Dengke raison d'être – gifts of a
slingshot and a rubber ball*

Fig. 5
Dave and Rachel demonstrating skateboarding skills

Fig. 6
*Buddhists prostrating themselves for
hundreds of miles to earn "karma merit"*

Fig. 7
Leprosy sufferer, Shintso, visited by John G, Glyn, Mel, Phil, Val and Marianne

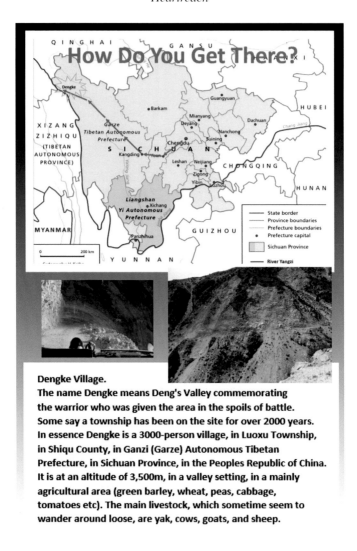

Dengke Village.
The name Dengke means Deng's Valley commemorating
the warrior who was given the area in the spoils of battle.
Some say a township has been on the site for over 2000 years.
In essence Dengke is a 3000-person village, in Luoxu Township,
in Shiqu County, in Ganzi (Garze) Autonomous Tibetan
Prefecture, in Sichuan Province, in the Peoples Republic of China.
It is at an altitude of 3,500m, in a valley setting, in a mainly
agricultural area (green barley, wheat, peas, cabbage,
tomatoes etc). The main livestock, which sometime seem to
wander around loose, are yak, cows, goats, and sheep.

Fig. 8
The journey to Dengke is sometimes fraught with danger

Fig. 9
*Couples who found romance through Project Dengke
including: John O and Val; Keith and Barbara;
Marc and Marion; Mel and Ci Ci; John and Sally;
John W and Kathy; Phil and Katherine.*

Fig. 10
*Cycling Hero, Michael Zhang, cycled
around the entire world to support us*

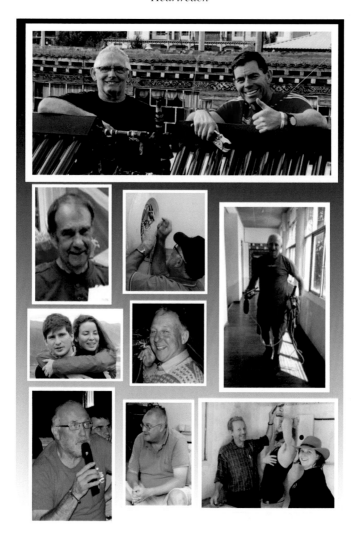

Fig. 11
The Engineering and Medical Team including:
John G and Phil M; David; Ben and Emily;
Phil B; Jim; Nigel; Charlotte; and Dave

Fig. 12
Geoff surprises the welder with two left-handed gloves,
plus DIY practitioners Jim, David, Glyn and Abigail

Fig. 13
Interpreters and key team members:
Tamar; Royal; David; Christine; Willow; Martin,
Stephanie; Sarah; Fiona; Ci Ci; Mary; Godfrey; Janet;
Sean; Phil B; Joan; Ray; Glyn; and Ruth

Fig. 14
The "Jacquelyne Richardson International Friendship Centre"
Dengke

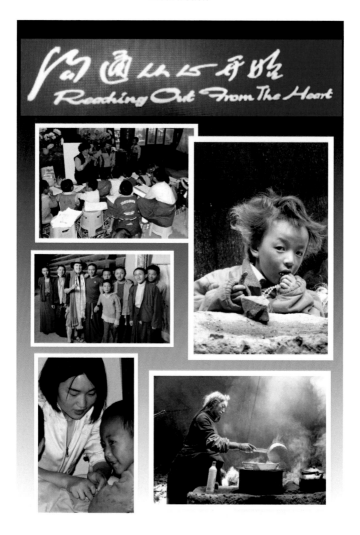

Fig. 15
Heartreach in Action:
Francesca; Rachel; Mel; and Pacific

Fig. 16
The "Xu Family" Tom, Phoebe,
Christina, James and Moses

Fig. 17
Ang Luo's delightful vegetarian restaurant in Kangding

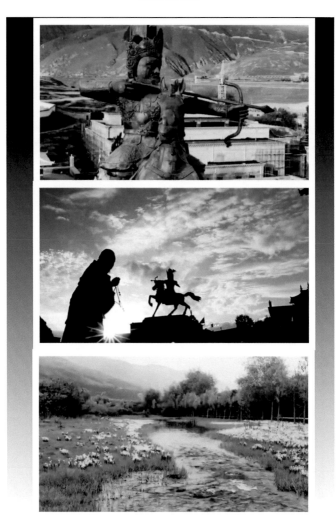

Fig. 18
Aerial views of Dengke

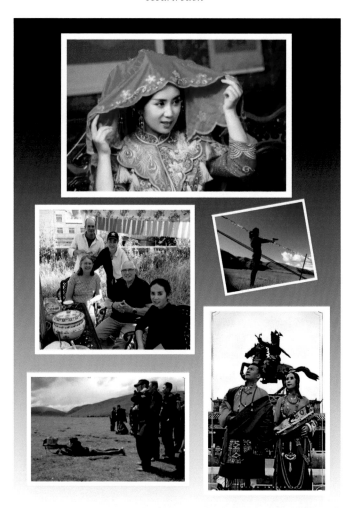

Fig. 19
Lhamu's wedding and training pictures

Fig. 20
Special participants:
Frank; D and K; Doreen; Nigel; Fiona B; Rigar and Mel

Fig. 21
*"Dusty Miller" and his water powered flour grinding mill
with John G and Glyn*

Fig. 22
Dengke views

Fig. 23
Close friends and supporters:
Mel; "old cook" Gou Guohua; Glyn; Michael;
David; Lily; and Sophie

Fig. 24
Prayer Warriors:
Gwen; Joyce; Jean M; Jean D; and Maureen;
plus singing duo brother and sister Laurence and Emily

Fig. 25
Sharing love and kindness to Shintso and friends:
Val; John O; Pacific; and Katie

Fig. 26
The Dengke marriage of Yang Ting and Ren Sa
(Wujin and Neega's youngest son)
– all the Team were invited

Fig. 27
An exotic and colourful celebration of Dengke history and culture – the Team were made guests of honour

Fig. 28
*"Crocodile" Carey teaching monks
and ministering to the Team*

Fig. 29
*Jim Wild heroically abseiled down the
Portsmouth Spinnaker Tower as a fundraiser,
surrounded by Alverstoke Evangelical Church supporters*

BOOKS BY REV ALEX JACOB, CEO OF CMJ

100 Days With Luke
In one hundred easy to digest studies, Alex Jacob opens up Luke. The one Gospel account written by a non-Jew, Luke speaks to Jewish people as much as anyone else! These short studies open up many questions about the Lordship of Jesus from his birth to his ascension.

Each day contains a passage from Luke, a brief reflection from the writer and finally a "to consider" question. Ideal for both private and group study. This material has been adopted as useful Lent Course material.

100 Days With Acts
A 'partner' volume to *100 Days With Luke*, this book carries on Luke's witness across a hundred day study period. Acts reflects the acts of the Holy Spirit, just as it reflects the acts of the apostles. Each day contains a passage from Acts, a brief reflection from the writer, and finally a "to consider" question. Ideal for both private and group study. Has also been adopted as useful Lent Course material.

60 Days With Romans (planned Q4-2020)
Using the same format as the 100-days studies (above), this shorter edition explores Romans. In much the same way, a very serviceable and incisive, biblically astute yet thoroughly accessible study. Investing in this series helps Christians build up a useful personal library that they will undoubtedly return to from time to time.

This series also makes life easier for the busy house group leader, or church leader, and can accompany a preaching series.

Christian Publications International

www.christian-publications-int.com